Leeds Tramcars

A Penny Ride To Town
1933-1950

LEEDS TRAMCARS

A PENNY RIDE TO TOWN

1933-1950

BRIAN RENDER

Wharncliffe Books

Plate 1: Car 272 at Sovereign Street Permanent Way Yard in 1935. Leeds City Transport.

Plate 2: The Leeds Coat of Arms. By permission of Leeds City Council, Strategic Policy Committee.

First Published in 2000 by
Wharncliffe Books
an imprint of
Pen and Sword Books Limited,
47 Church Street, Barnsley,
South Yorkshire. S70 2AS

Copyright © Brian Render

For up-to-date information on other titles produced under the
Wharncliffe imprint, please telephone or write to:

> **Wharncliffe Books**
> **FREEPOST**
> **47 Church Street**
> **Barnsley**
> **South Yorkshire S70 2BR**
> **Telephone (24 hours): 01226 - 734555**

ISBN: 1-871647-88-6

A CIP catalogue record of this book is available from the
British Library

Cover illustration: City Square in wartime emptiness.
Yorkshire Post

Printed in Great Britain by
Redwood Books, Trowbridge, Wiltshire

CONTENTS

To my parents who helped oil the wheels of ambition and to my wife Mabel who inspired me to improve and complete this story

Plate 3: Car 299, One of the 'magic two's' seen at Elland Road Football Ground on 19 March, 1938. H.B. Priestley/National Tramway Museum Collection.

6

INTRODUCTION

In 1991, a friend, together with David Lardge, then the Manager of the National Tramway Museum at Crich, Derbyshire, arranged, without my knowledge, a little nostalgic event for 3 November, to celebrate a birthday that I didn't want to admit to.

We arrived at Crich to be asked to board Leeds car 399 at Town End, which we did and I immediately went to sit at the front, offside of the saloon (inside) as I always tried to do in Leeds through the years in order to see-out-front and watch the driver, who, today was Colin Heaton, also from Leeds. Colin knew all about our visit.

From my seat I looked at the destination blinds inside 399. Much to my surprise they said 'Special Car'. Now, even in 1991, being on a car with these words on the blinds was wrong! (We had been well-disciplined in Leeds years ago). So when I asked David Lardge why the car was so indicated he replied with a smile, 'Why not! It's yours today'!!

And it was, too.

I had no answer to that and a little later, after Colin had taken 399 further up the line, he stopped the car and said to us, 'Now, only persons aged sixty-five today can drive this car.'

My mind flashed back fifty nine years to Harehills Corner and I was sitting in a similar car and watching the driver, wishing that he would do what Colin had just done!

What a surprise and what a day. What could I say to David Lardge and Colin Heaton or to my friend who were in on today's secret? Utter bliss!!

It wouldn't have been possible for me to have ridden on, much less drive 399 in 1933. Apart from my being only six years old, 399 would normally have been running on 5-Beeston from Harehills and would have travelled via Vicar Lane and Corn Exchange. My parents 'never went to Corn Exchange'.

Later on that day in 1991 Colin said to me,

Your memories of Leeds tramcars must go back a long way, especially as you went to work in the Head Office of Leeds Tramways. Why don't you write down what you remember about the trams and your interest in them from your early days?

In the following pages I have tried to convey how I grew up with the tramcars in Leeds, how Leeds Tramways affected my family's everyday life and how the trams made such an impression on my very young mind so that whilst still at school a determined ambition established itself that I would work amongst the trams after I left school.

How this would be carried out I had no idea at sixteen years of age, but as so often happens when one is determined to do something, a way is always found. A way was found in a manner I could never have imagined, especially as we were surrounded by wartime worries and restrictions.

This story is not another engineering treatise on tramcars, nor is it a 'nut and bolt counters' manual. It is not an historical survey of the Tramway facts of Leeds during the 1930s and 1940s.

It is a personal memoir.

During these years, the Tramway feelings, excitements, discoveries and ultimately Tramway work were facts of my daily life.

Now, in hindsight, those Tramway events and influences have become intimate, unforgettable personal memories. Therefore I make no apologies for portraying a very close affinity with Leeds trams and an even greater bias towards them. I have always treated them as 'my' trams and I continue to do so, even sixty years after the time to which this story relates.

Leeds trams gave me intense satisfaction and delight to behold them, to 'know' them personally by their sound and appearance, their name and number and their style, to travel on them and eventually to work for them. Memories of all the Leeds cars were permanently etched in my mind from the time when 399 was about seven years old, the Pivs were about six years old and when the Horsfields (P35s) were about two years old.

As a record of my excitements with the trams in Leeds, the story is as truthfully and passionately recalled as memory will allow. I just hope that my memory is not playing me any hidden tricks.

All opinions expressed herein are mine. They do not represent any official statements or policies made at the time or since.

May 1999
Brian Render

Plate 4: Cookridge Street about 1939 showing the YWCA, bus for Otley and three tramcars. Perhaps on a Saturday afternoon. Yorkshire Post.

Acknowledgements

Edgar Allen Trackwork, Sheffield; Appleby Business Services, Appleby-in-Westmorland; John Baxter Photography, Appleby-in-Westmorland; Brush Electrical Machines, Loughborough; W.A. Camwell/National Tramway Museum Collection; Keith Chadbourne, National Tramway Museum, Crich, Derbyshire; Colab Ltd, Coventry; A.A. Daggett, Works Superintendent, Kirkstall Works, Leeds City Transport; Bernard Donald, York; Mr Downey, Depot Foreman, Torre Road, Leeds City Transport; D.M. Francis, The National Library of Wales, Aberystwyth; Frank Graves, Appleby-in-Westmorland; Mrs Ruth Harris, Principal Archivist, West Yorkshire Archives Service, Wakefield; Colin Heaton, National Tramway Museum, Crich, Derbyshire; Geoffrey Hilditch, Torbay; Albert Howells, Depot Foreman, Swinegate Depot, Leeds City Transport; Steve Johnson, Optare Ltd, Cross Gates, Leeds; Brian Lancaster, Kendal; David Lardge, Manager, National Tramway Museum, Crich, Derbyshire; Leeds City Council, Strategic Policy Committee, per Ian Walton; Leeds City Transport Department; Leeds Transport Historical Society; The Principal Librarian, Leeds Local and Family History Library; Leicestershire Record Office; National Tramway Museum, Crich, Derbyshire; Nottingham University Photographic Unit; Ordnance Survey, Southampton; Mr Pegram, Yardman, Swinegate Depot, Leeds City Transport; Stuart G. Pickford, Caterham; A.S. Pope, Supertram Co-ordinator, Leeds City Council; John Porter, Outhgill, Kirkby Stephen; H.B. Priestley/National Tramway Museum Collection; Prontaprint, Carlisle and Leeds; Mr and Mrs Arthur Render, Leeds; Michael Seymour, Cambridge; Paul Shepherd, Reading Buses; J. Soper, Leeds; Sports and General Press Agency, London; Keith Terry, Leeds; Mrs Rosemary Thacker, Librarian, National Tramway Museum, Crich, Derbyshire; J. Wade, Depot Foreman, Swinegate Depot, Leeds City Transport; West Yorkshire Archives Service, Sheepscar, Leeds; West Yorkshire Passenger Transport Executive, Leeds; Wetherall, Green & Smith, Leeds; Glynn Wilton, Photographer, National Tramway Museum, Crich, Derbyshire; Yard staff of Swinegate Depot, Leeds City Transport; 'Yorkshire Post', Leeds.

Bibliography

Bowtell, Harold, *Lesser Railways of the Yorkshire Dales*, 1991; Clay, Ewart W., *The Leeds Police*, 1975; Coates, D.M., *Bradford City Tramways*, 1882-1950, 1984; Crowther, C.H., *Trams in Leeds, Modern Tramway*, August, 1969; Glass's Guide Service, *Glass's Index of Registration Numbers, 1929-1965*; Hilditch, G.G., *Looking at Buses*, 1979; Leeds and District Transport News, *A Fleet History of Leeds City Transport*, 1969; Mack R.F., *Leeds City Tramways, A Pictorial Souvenir*, 1972; Mack, R.F., *Buses in Leeds, Past, Present and Future*, 1974; Proudlock, Noel, *Leeds, A History of its Tramways*, 1991; Soper, J., *Leeds Transport, Volume 1. 1830-1902*, 1985; Soper, J., *Leeds Transport, Volume 2. 1902-1931*, 1996; Terry, Keith, *Early Memories of the Oldest Trams in Leeds During the Last War*, 1993; Twidale, Graham H.E., *A Nostalgic Look at Leeds Trams Since 1950*, 1991; Ward, Lock and Co. Ltd., *Wonder Book of Science*, 1936; Wiseman, R.J.S., *British Tramways in Pictures, No. 4, Leeds*, 1980; 'Yorkshire Post', *City of Leeds Guide*, 1947; Young, Andrew D, *Leeds Trams 1932-1959*, 1972.

Chapter One

A CHILDHOOD OF TRAMCARS

In the musical *Half a Sixpence*, Tommy Steele sang, 'What a Picture! What a Photograph!' Long before this phrase was ever put to music, I might, as a very young lad and if I had been able to put words together properly, have said something similar about each of three photographs my mother took of Roundhay Road and Harehills Road in 1921/1922. She took them out of interest, no doubt as ordinary 'record shots', but they are now, 70-odd years later, very important views of history.

One view is taken at Trinity Methodist Church looking up Roundhay Road towards Shepherds Lane, with two tramcars in the distance. Another view is taken from near Clock Buildings looking up Roundhay Road towards Blackburn's aircraft factory in late 1921 or early 1922, just before work started to move the tram-tracks to the reservation. Two tramcars are just visible. The third view is of Harehills Road from Gipton School towards Roundhay Road and shows the overhead-line poles between the tram tracks. (See map 3, p. 45)

All three photographs show the little area of Leeds with which my family was familiar, particularly as my first school was Gipton. Neither road has changed very much over the years, but the trams have gone and have been replaced by queues of parked and moving cars and folk have changed too.

My mother, born in 1892, was the person most likely to have been responsible for sowing the seeds of my interest in Leeds tramcars. Very obviously, the interest had been firmly planted by the time I was

Plate 5: Roundhay Road at Trinity Methodist Church, in 1922 with two tramcars visible. The lady on the left is my maternal grandmother, Mrs Eliza Ingham who would be 61 years old here. Mrs Annie Render.

Plate 6: Harehills Road and Gipton School in 1922, with the overhead lines on poles between the tracks. Mrs Annie Render.

six years old because the earliest thing I can remember about Leeds cars is that one day in July 1933, my father cycled home from his work in Leeds (Leeds was always spoken about as being a different place from Harehills in those days), perhaps a little faster than normal that day.

As he came in the back door after putting his cycle in the shed he said to me, 'There's a new tram out in Leeds'. I remember asking him, 'What number is it?' and he replied, '255 and it's a beauty. It's for Middleton.'

It is coincidental that 255 entered passenger service in Leeds in July just before the visit to Leeds in August 1933 by King George V to open the Civic Hall.

Certainly 255 was the king of Leeds tramcars!

I must have known something about the other cars in Leeds in order to have been concerned about the number. I recently found a nursery rhyme composed and written by my mother in January, 1929 which records that at the age of two years two months, 'Brian was keenly interested in all the people and other things mentioned' in the rhyme. Some of those things were, 'bobbins and buckets and motor cars, books and buses and tramcars too'. The video called 'Leeds Trams', produced by Online Video and Leeds Transport Historical Society, also triggered some deep-down memories.

Now in those early days, I didn't know where Middleton was, because the furthest my parents would go was the occasional ride into Leeds and back on the tram, or, as a treat, up to Roundhay Park where many major events were held. Otherwise one walked or cycled when of age so to do. In spite of constant pleading, my parents would not take me down to Leeds just to look for 255 or any other car, they

Plate 7: Car 400 - My favourite tramcar when new in 1925. Compare plate 119.
Leeds City Transport.

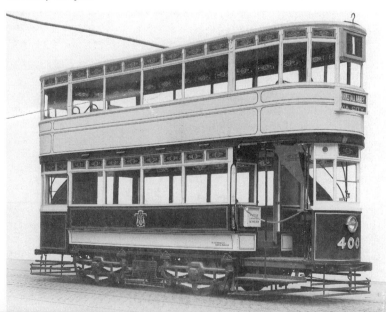

Plate 8: Roundhay Road twoards Oakwood in 1922, just before the tram tracks were moved from the left hand side of the road to a reservation behind the wall on the right. Mrs Annie Render.

could just not afford that.

Since completing the 'first writing' of this story, some old family photographs have been unearthed and catalogued. These have confirmed that at least once a year, between 1927 and 1937, my parents took me to Leeds to the Queens Arcade for a birthday photograph.

On these occasional visits to Leeds on the tram, we must have gone to Briggate. But by what type of tram? Not until 1933/34 would I have realised that some trams had 'roofs on' and some did not. The cars with 'roofs on' were 'waterproof', those that I thought were not had open top-ends that were 'empty'.

In hindsight perhaps these were subconscious memories. Because it was beyond my ability at the time to do anything more than look, 60 years later such things are historically infuriating.

'Waterproof' was my newly-taught word at that time for a totally-enclosed car. 'Empty' top-ends was a little lad's description of cars with open-ended top decks. They would be 'empty' because nobody would sit there in cold weather.

One of these 'waterproof' cars was 400, a Pivotal car. In 1934, 400 would only have been 8 years old, but it was the only one, so my parents told me, where I could stand at the front, upstairs and be held tight and look out of the small window between the 'top-box' and the 'bottom-box' - Bliss! (Plate 7). Rather like 399 sixty years later at Crich. So my parents would wait to see if 400 was about in 'No 3' area, i.e. Harehills Corner, Clock Buildings towards Blackburn's Factory. If the 'magic' car did happen to be about then we would wait for it to come on round from Clock Buildings and I would try to be first upstairs to 'my' window.

Car 400 came to be known very quickly by myself as 'Aunty Martin's car,' because of a friend of my mother who lived in the London area and whose surname was Martin. I was told in the fashion of the day that I could call her 'Aunty' out of familiar politeness. However, Aunty Martin worked at Pontings in London and 400 had an advertisement for Pontings on one end of the car on the panelling just above the driver's right-hand-side, on the curving portion of the end. I actually remember where but not when this name was bestowed on 400. The car had stopped at Roundhay Road 'Parade' stop and my mother and I were on the opposite side of the road in front of Harehills Cinema when this advertisement was pointed out to me by my mother. The name has lasted for ever as a first example for me of 'association of ideas.'

I find it alternately strange and normal that 400 is in constant memory, my favourite car and that it was looked upon with such excitement. (Later I had a favourite bus too! It was FNW 46, fleet number 76). No 399, albeit the next-numbered car to 400, was like many others of that 'build' that ran on 5-Beeston and associated routes, but was always 'let-go' if it was coming from Clock Buildings because it would be on Beeston via Vicar Lane and Corn Exchange.

Now, 60 years later, 400 has gone and 399 is immaculate in its original primrose at the National Tramway Museum at Crich. We always ride on it on visits to Crich and we cannot now go to Corn Exchange! But whilst riding on 399, in my imagination I am back on route '3' on 400.

To visually span the last 60-odd years, I have over my mantelpiece a large print, by courtesy of Glynn Wilton, photographer at Crich, of 399 'as restored' in 1991. Next to it and of the same size is a print of

Plate 9: Bus No. 76, FNW 46. My favourite bus at Torre Road Garage on 9 May 1944. Note the wartime khaki paint, white edging and headlamp masks. Author.

Plate 10: Car 255 - 'The King of Leeds Tramcars' when new in 1933. Leicestershire Records Office.

400 in 1927, allegedly 'as built'. The photographers were the Leeds firm of Charles Pickard. It is stated in some books that 400 was put into service in December 1925, but this photograph, dated 1927, shows the car in immaculate condition, typically an 'as built' view. Perhaps the print itself was prepared in 1927 because the L.C.T. rubber stamp dated 1927 is on the rear of the original copy.

In 1933 one went to Leeds (Briggate) by a 4-Kirkstall or a 1-Lawnswood car from Harehills Corner, never by a 5-Beeston car to Vicar Lane or Corn Exchange, so I presume that my parents must have taken me down Karnac Road to the 'Parade', i.e. at Roundhay Road/Harehills Road junction, in order to get the tram to Leeds. The 'Parade' was a wide area of early pedestrianisation between the shops and roadway on the Potternewton side of Roundhay Road. The shops on the other sides of this junction were set back too so the whole area seemed spacious. The tram-tracks here formed a double junction, one pair coming in from Harehills Road, one pair along Roundhay Road from Leeds and the third pair coming from Clock Buildings at the bottom of Easterly Road.

Cars did not normally run through from Harehills Road on to Roundhay Road, except when special events were being held at Roundhay Park, mostly at weekends. Cars on the 'shuttle run'

Plate 11: Cars 394 and 367 at 11-Harehills Road terminus in 1938. Roundhay Road in the background. H.B. Priestley/National Tramway Museum Collection.

between Roundhay and Harehills would turn into Harehills Road and reverse on the cross-over at the Harehills Sorting Office of the General Post Office. Normally the crossover was the terminus of 11-Harehills Road from Dewsbury Road.

From Karnac Road, before going to the tram-stop near Harehills Cinema, we would always turn left for a few yards into Harehills Road to examine James Frew's Sports and Model Railways shop. Mr Frew always had O-gauge Hornby trains in the window. At Christmas-time a track was laid in the window and the trains ran round the flat area. Most exciting! There were no other gauges then and one day, possibly in 1937, there, in the centre of the window display was a magnificent O-gauge model of L.M.S. locomotive 6201 - 'Princess Elizabeth', in a maroon (Hornby) box, for five pounds, five shillings - and nobody could afford it!

Sometimes we walked down to the bottom of Milan Road to Harehills Road so that I could see possibly two cars at the Sorting Office crossover. One car would be ready to come back over the crossover and start off up the slope to the Congregational Church - the first stop - on its way to 9-Dewsbury Road via Beckett Street and Corn Exchange. I didn't know where Dewsbury Road was at that period. The other car would then drift down over the 'bottom' trailing points which would 'CHLONK.... CHLONK' as the point blades sprung back, after each pair of wheels had gone through, into the 'cross-over' position.

Then we would watch the Conductor as he bent down at the side of the car to unhook the bamboo pole from its usually secure position. He raised the pole to near vertical and hooked it on to the trolley-boom near the wheel and walked round the car, holding the bamboo pole in both hands to reposition the trolley-wheel under the overhead wire to allow the car to trail the trolley-boom to Dewsbury Road. This description is written in hindsight, as although we watched the procedure often, no 'technical terms' were known to us. This procedure was carried out at all termini, except where trolley-reversers were installed - another subject beyond my 'ken' at that time.

At this Sorting Office location the road surface was of setts, sometimes referred to as 'cobblestones' and these were fairly uneven and sometimes slippy. Woe betide any conductor who tripped or slipped with a trolley boom at the end of his bamboo pole. If the conductor 'lost' the bamboo pole and, as a result, the boom flew up to a vertical position above the car roof (taking the bamboo pole with it), it was immediately necessary to call out the overhead-line derrick and gang from their base at Crown Point.

The conductor concerned would not know where to put himself during this time and his stomach would probably have dropped altogether when he would be told that 'Mr Gill (or his predecessor) wanted to see him - NOW'

Along with a lot more tramcar noises, the sound of those points 'CHLONKING' back to position has stayed in my mind for ever.

Perhaps when you visit Crich Tramway Museum you may see a person standing fairly close to a set of trailing points. Please do not disturb him, for he will be listening for the points to 'CHLONK' as a car comes up from Town End, his mind at the same time going back 60 years to that crossover at Harehills Road Sorting Office

Many tramway noises from my early days in Leeds have remained just below the surface of my memory. Our house was in Milan Road, (See map 3, p. 45) two thirds of the way up from Harehills Road. From our front door and when conditions allowed, provided that the tingalairy man wasn't in the street, I could hear a car feed-up after leaving the cross-over at the Sorting Office until it reached the section-point at the bottom of Luxor Avenue. (At that time I didn't know that a car did 'feed-up' or what a 'section-point' was)

The driver would throw-off, coast over the break and immediately feed-up again into parallel to take the car up to the first stop at Harehills Place. At the point of feeding-up again the noise would tell me what type of car was coming up i.e. a 'Pivotal' or a 'non-waterproof' car, say. Also, on occasions a Horsfield (P.35) and later the Hull cars would come up. Sometimes, as I got to know the cars better and because of some side-panel treatment or other individual distinguishing marks, it was possible to identify which particular car it was as it went past the bottom of Milan Road at right-angles to my line of sight. I can still 'hear' those cars in that location.

On a visit to the Tramway Museum at Crich in October 1992, I was told by a certain very well-known tramway 'encyclopaedia' from Leeds that, in 1942 an ex-London HR2, 277 no less, actually travelled up Harehills Road past the bottom of Milan Road to Stanley Road, en route from Roundhay to Leeds, having been deviated due to trackwork repairs. To have seen 277 in such a position would have made my eyes pop in disbelief. Even then I was getting to know that certain cars never went on certain routes. Well, hardly ever.

In 1979 when I was, appropriately, living in Beeston, Nottingham, on a quiet evening I 'heard' a tramcar of the 300-342 'non-waterproof' type start up from Beeston Square and drive towards the bottom of the road where I lived. The noise was absolutely L.C.T. as though one of those cars had escaped from Torre Road or Low Fields Road and had hidden away for years. No 324 did, I believe. Unfortunately my imaginings were shattered when a custom-built motor cycle shot past me at the road-end. It was, nevertheless, an indication of how Leeds cars have never left my thoughts.

Another recent instance of personal rememberings of Leeds car numbers and images has been provided during the preparation of an index to my Photographic Collection of Ffestiniog History, now in the National Library of Wales at Aberystwyth. Many of the volumes in this collection have page numbers from 1 to 500 or 600. These numbers are easily remembered by association with similar Leeds tramcar numbers. Perhaps I should explain. The page numbers of any volume in the collection that brought back immediate individual tramcar recall were between 1 and 445. The numbers 446 to 477 brought back the thought, 'Oh! Yes, those were the Hull cars!' Those pages between 501 and 590 or so reminded me that the 'London cars' were numbered thus. Page 600 was always the Sunderland car and pages 601 and 602 only meant single-deckers. The all-important numbers were between 1 and 445. The others didn't matter so much, they were not my Leeds trams.

In all the years since 1941, i.e. long before I actually found the mystery cars 283 to 299 and, indeed, right up to the present time any balcony car whose number started with the 'magic two' was of exciting interest. These cars were 'old cars' and were, and still are, thought of with excited reverence! So when the page numbers corresponding to these cars came up, my mind temporarily blotted out the index in hand and I was back in Torre Road Top Shed (Chapter 6) on the day I found the cars with the 'magic twos'

Even today in church when the hymn board is put up before the service starts, invariably the hymn numbers are between 1 and 500. If one of the hymns happens to be 296 then again I am immediately 'transported' back to 1942 to Torre Road Top Shed, at the same time enjoying my favourite hymn - 'Guide me 0 thou great Jehovah'.

Back now to Roundhay Road at Harehills in 1933. Having watched what happened to the cars as they stopped at the No.11 terminus we would progress to Harehills Corner where no end of cars would be passing up and down Roundhay Road. We could see from here to past Copgrove Road for any 1-Lawnswood cars coming from Roundhay or any 4-Kirkstall cars too, and any other cars coming from Clock Buildings/Easterly Road, which was the terminus for 3-Harehills Road cars. Thus we could see in ample time if 400 was anywhere about. If, after a short time, there was no sign of the tram we would admit defeat and board any tram going to Briggate. (Never to Corn Exchange, you know. I never did find out why not!)

Thereby hangs another tale, because whichever car we got on, if my father was with us it was 'upstairs'. If my mother and granny were taking me then it was 'inside', not downstairs. If we went upstairs then all the seats faced forwards except those fixed to the sides/ends of the cars near the stairwell. Does anyone remember the sound of the wooden seat-backs of the Pivotals being swung over at a terminus? Those seat-backs had a totally different sound from the seat-backs on the Beeston cars or the P.35s or the balcony cars.

If possible I was allowed a seat to myself to look out of the window on the nearside of the car down into shops or on to the roofs of motor cars and other vehicles. 1 could imagine then that they were Dinky Toys and how my fingers would grasp the vehicle to push it along realistically.

If we went 'inside' on the Pivotals or on any of the older cars, then everybody faced one another on the long seats on either side of the car, like 399 at Crich. Exceptions to this generalisation were cars 44 and 89 which had forward-facing seats downstairs. Of course, I had to try to sit at the front of the saloon at the window next to the driver's platform to see-out-front and watch the driver.

A thought about the 'front-end' of a tramcar. Both ends of any Leeds tramcar were identical, except for being numbered No.1 End and No.2 End, to assist in maintenance routines etc, When a car was driven into service, the driver's end became the front end, obviously. The driver's end was always forbidden to passengers (except when boarding at Briggate barriers).

When a car reached a terminus, the end that was the driver's became the conductor's or passengers' end. The other end that was the passengers' end now became the front or the driver's end and was again forbidden to passengers. The driver's end was always the end on which I wanted to travel and never could. However, I could always imagine that I was the driver by standing, very briefly, facing backwards with my hands on the controller handle and brake handle during that short time between coming downstairs and actually getting off the car at a normal stop.

The driver's end was the exciting end giving a totally different experience to the front end of any other vehicle. On the rare occasions in later years when I was allowed to ride on this end, it really was (and still is) an exciting thing to do. To actually drive a Leeds tramcar in Leeds was even more exciting. To drive a Leeds tramcar at the National Tramway Museum at Crich is just as exciting 60 years later.

Spare a thought for the hundreds of drivers through the years whose job it was to drive tramcars all day, sometimes on a car with no windscreen and who were therefore exposed to all weathers. It wasn't much better really for drivers of cars without platform doors, even with windscreens. That's one of the reasons why the Horsfields (P.35s) were looked on with such pleasure, they had doors on!

Not so exciting for those drivers and not so comfortable as we were when we rode on the cars. We would board and sit or stand in it, pay a fare for so doing and get off where we wished. The driver, having stopped for us to get off, drove off and disappeared from our view and our thoughts.

Plate 12: The top deck of Car 400 to show the wooden seats with reversible backs, standard in 1925. Leeds City Transport.

Nobody gave much thought to the driver and conductor until we came to get on a car again. I wonder if there are any tram crews left and what stories they could tell?

Since 1990, over thirty years after the trams ceased to run in Leeds, I have often talked to people who were born after 1959 and who never knew what trams were. Many questions were asked, many were easy to answer and were easily understood by the questioner.

One question that I could not believe I was hearing was: 'How did you steer the trams?' A daft question? A mickey-taking question? No! A genuine question by a young person who reasoned that the trams ran on public roads like any other vehicles: they looked like the present-day double-deck buses (well, some did!) and buses were steered, so why not trams?

After giving the answer with as straight a face as possible, I began to wonder why, even in my early years up to six, say, I had always known that the trams ran on the rails that were laid-in and were flush with the road surface (usually). We put pennies on the rails to be flattened. We saw cyclists get their wheels in the grooves. We saw and heard the points at a junction move with a 'chlonk' and sometimes water would splash up and over us in heavy rain if we were too close to the car that changed the points. We understood the cars were on rails. It was part of the city life! The cars derailed sometimes and that was exciting, especially to watch them being pulled or pushed back on to the track.

Perhaps if in 1995 I had asked the young person who had asked me about how the trams were steered: 'How do you clean *Windows '95*'? I should have seen the pitying look on his face.

To return once again to about 1933 at Harehills Corner. Occasionally during our few minutes wait at the barrier. near the Harehills Cinema, a car would come from Roundhay direction with 'Special Car' on the destination blind with the route number and via panels blank. Everybody in those days knew about 'Special Cars' and that any attempt to board a car so indicated was absolutely forbidden. In any case there was a chain in a leather tube across the rear platform to prevent unauthorised 'jumping-on'.

In this 'Year of 255' when we were to take the tram to Leeds, another type of car would come from Clock Buildings, either from Roundhay or Easterly Road. This car was of a smoother shape up to my height and I could see my reflection in the flat sides as the car came slowly past us to a stop in the middle of the road at the Harehills Cinema stop. Actually the barriers were nearer Whittaker's Shoe Shop. In order to board the cars at most stops, all intending passengers had to step out into the road for a distance of about fifteen feet and any motor vehicles had to wait. Imagine that happening in 1999! On these smoother cars, about my height or a little below my eye-level, was a name that, although it was on all the cars, did not mean much to me then. I vaguely wondered who the person was who could have his name on every Leeds car. He must be a very 'lucky' person! The name was W. Vane Morland, General Manager and Engineer. This gentleman's name has always meant to me 'Leeds Tramways' (never mind the buses!). He was Leeds Tramways! Ten years later when I went to work in Leeds City Transport this impression was totally confirmed. Having boarded this car, which was a P.35 or Horsfield (which name was unknown to me then), I found that the seat arrangement inside was very different from the older cars. There were double seats on one side of the saloon and single seats on the other all facing forwards, except two seats next to the driver's platform window where I could still try to get to see-out-front. The dark-maroon seat-covering was cold at first to a short-trousered young lad, but why worry, there were a lot more levers, handles and wheels to look at and wonder how they worked on this type of car. I didn't know how they worked on any type of car, but I always wanted to know. It was also apparent, even to me, that the driver did not have to be winding the large handle on his right at all on these cars. He operated a small handle with only a short movement in front of him and this car had doors on the driver's platform too. In my thoughts, 'this was quite a good car!' I didn't know these cars by any other reference than 151 to 254 and that took a very long time to observe and learn. When eventually I realised that 254 was the last number of this type of car, I remembered thinking, 'that's next to 255, so whatever does 255 look like?!'

The Horsfield car that was just that bit different from the others was 158 (Plate 14). There always seems to be one car that is on its own for whatever reason. In 158's case it was different because of a further white lining that had been added inside the gold lining on the front and side panels of blue on the lower deck - the panels that I could see my reflection in! This white lining was probably on the upper deck too, but that was too high up for me then. Of course, other Horsfield cars may have had this or similar treatments, but my little world of trams was limited to what I saw around Harehills on routes 1,3,4,5,9 and 11.

Then one day in early 1935 we were down at the tram-stop at Harehills Cinema and were waiting to get on a car to Leeds when we were very surprised to see a car coming from Clock Buildings direction which was an entirely different colour - pale blue - to any car we had seen before. You see, in spite of hearing about 255 from my father, I had never seen it or any other Middleton car and if 255's colour was ever thought about at all, it could have been assumed to have been similar to 151 to 254. I did not learn that 255 and, indeed, all the other Middleton cars were painted light blue until I saw some of them for the first time in 1940. My father's 'intelligence network' hadn't cottoned-on to tramcar colours.

So what was this strange car with a V-front and an easy-to-read destination blind (for Granny) and a window above it? Most exciting. We must get on this car. We did and we went upstairs. I suppose even Granny would have been a little excited about this car in order to go upstairs. She didn't have any trouble in this respect because the stairs were

Plate 13: Mr W. Vane Morland, General Manager and Engineer, Leeds City Transport. Transport World.

straight with handrails. The handrails at the doorway as we got on were shiny black, not brass as on the older cars. Once upstairs, joy of joys, at the front we could sit in forward-facing seats with warm coverings which 'whooshed' when sat on and we could see-out-front all round! By Jove, this was a posh car and it went to Briggate and was then going on to a place called Headingley. On the top rail above the front windows on the top deck was a transfer that said, 'Built by Leeds City Transport' and the number 272 was just above this in the same style of numbers that were on the destination boxes of other cars

Later on in 1935, my father told me that there were another two of these cars and that they were 273 and 274. When I eventually saw these two cars I noticed that 272 had a slightly different front shape to these two. To my little-boy mind then and indeed ever since, 272 had a much more 'come-and-ride-on-me' look about it as against a prim and proper 'Lawnswood - look' about the other two. That is hindsight, I suppose, because I didn't know where or what Lawnswood was at that time. These three cars were always on the Lawnswood/Roundhay/Moortown (1, 3 and 2) routes and so we saw

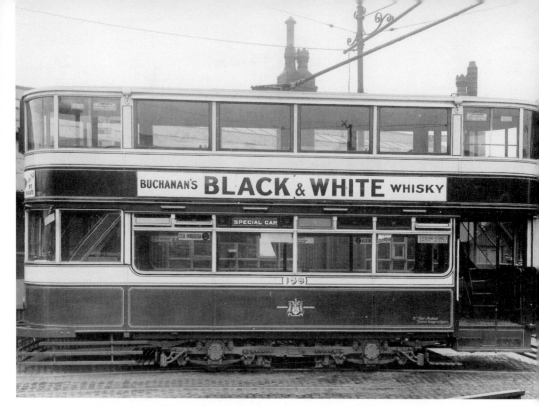

Plate 14: Car 158 - a Horsfield or P.35 seen in Sovereign Street Permanent Way Yard about 1933. Leeds City Transport.

a lot of them at Harehills. The driver had a seat in his own cabin. He must have appreciated that as no other cars that I had seen had a seat for the driver. Oh! The three cars had doors-on too The phrase 'that car has doors-on', came to refer to a car that I/we thought was up-to-date or posh or both.

In spite of 272, 273 and 274, we always looked for 400 when going to Leeds or when waiting in the Barriers in Briggate, or at Lewis's further up Briggate opposite the Paramount Picture House. It was always such a triumph if 400 happened to be on No.3, and we were able to ride on it. It was not until 1943 when I went to work at Leeds Tramways that I learned that 400 was about one year older than myself.

A sideways thought about the trams at Christmas-time between 1934 and 1938 when pantomimes were on in Leeds, but particularly at the Grand Theatre in New Briggate where 'Aladdin' was often the attraction. We would leave home at Harehills and I would be taken on the tram down to Leeds to the tramstop at the Grand Theatre AT NIGHT. An especial treat for a youngster in those days. The car we travelled on would most likely be a Pivotal on the journey to Leeds and I recall thinking how bright it all was and as our car came 'up and over' New Briggate the lights from all the shops, street-lights and decorations made everywhere almost like daylight. Probably all this was accentuated by so many people also going to the Theatre. My lasting impression is of a very exciting time.

Another thing about this time that I saw were the words 'POSTAL CAR' in red wound into position in the 'via' part of the destination indicator box (see car 132 in Plate 29). When 'Postal Car' was up a post box was carried on the car which then served as a travelling public post box. I have no idea of the start or the finish of this service, neither did I remember about it until I was able to obtain a copy of Mr W.A. Camwell's classic photograph of cars standing outside Stanley Road depot in 1939. Car 132 shows 'Postal Car' under the 'planted' destination - '14-Pudsey' up.

After the Pantomime was over - everybody was so sorry to leave - the whole audience spilled out from the Grand Theatre, down New Briggate to Lewis's and added to the crowd at the tram-stops. The whole of Briggate was lit up at this time and I think the cars had coloured light-bulbs in some cases, all serving to make a night trip a memorable occasion.

A secret hope on my part, even on such an exciting night out, was that 400 might come up Briggate - we could see the cars at the 'Barriers' and hear them easily from Lewis's. I wonder what the persons then in Swinegate Depot would have said had they known when they allocated 400 to a particular duty that their so-doing would 'make the day' of some unknown youngster in Harehills. It makes my day, 60 years later, to think about 400 as I write this.

After our theatre visit and once we had left Lewis's I remember saying to my parents, 'See if I can tell you where we are in the

Plate 15: The top deck (upper saloon) of Car 272 as new in 1935. Leeds City Transport.

darkness and with my eyes shut by the sound of the car', as we passed the Dispensary along and down North Street towards Golden Cross and Sheepscar and up Roundhay Road to Spencer Place and the Gaiety (Gathorne Terrace) to Whitfield Street, (St.Aidan's Church). Many a time I was wrong but it was enjoyable and good training for later life. This was a night that I was allowed to be up and out, late!

My parents also took me with them to the Grand Theatre whenever Gilbert and Sullivan's 'Gondoliers' or 'The Mikado' were to be performed. This was another exciting night-trip on the tram to town and back. The combination of musical magic, Gilbert and Sullivan, the D'Oyly Carte, the Grand Theatre and Leeds trams always evokes special memories. Thoughts of any one of these four bring to mind the other three.

Before the war the Arena below the Mansion at Roundhay Park was the location for the Tattoo, an earlier and smaller open-air version of the present-day Royal Tournament at Earls Court. Lots of exciting items, many guns, the 'storming of San Sebastian' etc.

My parents took me to see this event when I was probably about 7 years old. We walked down to Roundhay Road Parade tram stop where lots of cars were going to Roundhay Park. Some were shuttling back and forth from the Park to Harehills Road Sorting Office crossover.

At Roundhay Park Gates (Canal Gardens), throngs of tramcars from both directions were unloading people who would walk to the Arena and position themselves on Hill 60, the slope on the West side of the Arena, to watch the Tattoo.

Once the display was over the wide tarmac drive to the Park Gates was solid with folk queuing for a tram back home. All the tracks at the Park Gates were packed with tramcars - two tracks loading for Harehills and Town and one the other way to Moortown, etc. The cars were nearly all 'waterproof' ones and the track nearest the queuing barriers had a constantly-moving line of cars which were being added to by those reversing at Canal Gardens. These cars came down the middle track too so that the bottom cars on each line could load simultaneously.

What excitement to see all those cars together, never mind the Tattoo. It was another exciting night event for a young lad, but I didn't take any notes or numbers. Frustration, says me, 60 years later.

In September 1935 my parents took me to see the first L.N.E.R. streamlined locomotive 2509 'Silver Link' when it was new and on show at the railway yard in South Accommodation Road (always known later as 'South Accomm'). My memory of this day is only of two things. The tram-tracks in South Accomm. at the railway yard entrance towards Easy Road were double round a left-hand curve below and close to a wall. The rest was single track and loops. The double track next to the wall may have been a loop too, of course. This visit was another bit of tramway 'education', though I had no idea of what was at either end of this tram route and I have no recollection of the journey from Harehills to Leeds to Hunslet Road or the reverse, more's the pity. But we must have gone to the Corn Exchange or Briggate to change cars. Did not the cars that traversed South Accomm go to Lower Wortley? If so, where would we change in Leeds? This route closed in 1936 and cars from Lower Wortley went in the direction of York Road from then on, so even when I got to know Leeds tram routes better in 1943, I could never find much information about this somewhat obscure route. However the other point of memory is that 'Silver Link' had a corridor tender which we could walk through - a very new idea at that time.

There was another remote route that I only vaguely knew about because my parents sometimes spoke about it. We never had reason to use the route which was 29-Domestic Street, similar in character to South Accommodation Road and which branched off the Elland Road route into Holbeck. Cars from Domestic Street went across town as 30-Victoria Road, Hyde Park, an area opposite in character to Holbeck. I think the only reason my parents would mention it was because of its nearness to Holbeck Feast, a most famous Fair in those days.

It may be coincidental, but cars travelling from Domestic Street to Victoria Road passed close to the location of another well-known Leeds Fair - Woodhouse Feast. For the conductors on this route, winding on the route number from 29 to 30 and back to 29 at the termini was probably one of the easier parts of their job. The Domestic Street tracks from Elland Road were abandoned in late 1937, some years before I had a bike and was able to explore Leeds. Incidentally, Leeds Tramways never had a route 28. I wonder why?

Thinking about abandoned tracks, I wonder if the tracks in South Accomm. are still in situ under present surfaces? I always think that seeing or finding tram-tracks of abandoned tram routes is such a sadly final discovery that the feeling is of total frustration!

The single track by the side of Low Fields Road until recently was still there and showing through the covering-up material. It was enough to make any tram-person weep. Fancy, 70 cars in line down that roadside! Now, even Low Fields Road is cut in two by a new road but the memories are still there and so are the football crowds that the cars could shift far better than anything else on four wheels!

By 1935 I was beginning to take note of things like those maker's transfers, i.e. 'Brush', of Falcon Works, Loughborough and 'English Electric', Dick, Kerr Works, Preston. The former was a short-word design and the latter a longer scroll type transfer. Both distinctive, they were usually on the destination blind door upstairs on cars and on the left-hand side bulkhead inside the cars.

One could see these transfers whichever the direction of travel and they became firmly embedded in the mind, rather like some television advertisements today (if you let them) The item that I didn't know about until 1943 was the date that was to be found on one of the risers of the stairs on the platform at one end of every car and sometimes covered up by the conductor's coat. This date was the last time the car had been given a full repaint. Keith Terry knew about these dates and has been able to deduce much information about the 'lives' of the balcony cars as a result of noting every date on every car, but we didn't know about each other's parallel tram interests until later.

Also by 1935 the Middleton cars had all arrived in Leeds and 273 and 274 were in service later that year. I was aware, courtesy of father, of these two cars, but as we never went anywhere near Corn Exchange and very rarely near Lower Briggate I was not likely to see any of those Middleton cars.

In 1936 my father and mother and two friends became members of a tennis club, the courts of which were at Lawnswood, near the tram terminus. Of course, I was taken too and in a motor car!! The car was a square-back-and-sides (with fabric) Austin 12, registration number MP 6215 (always said sixty-two, fifteen). I was allowed to sit on my father's knees and I remember the huge steering wheel with an inner ring and lots of levers on it. It was a big thrill to ride in a motor car in those days.

When my parents were due to play, our route from Harehills was up Harehills Lane to Chapeltown Road and across it. But wait a moment! There's a big building just up there, as we crossed over Chapeltown Road, with overhead wires going into a high door. Father said that it must be Chapeltown 'tram-sheds'. Then we were past and up Potternewton Lane and down to Meanwood.

I had not been anywhere round here before and both parents were giving me a running commentary during the cross town journey so that I should be aware of districts in Leeds that I had only heard spoken about. Now, we had crossed the 2-Chapeltown/ Moortown route and I had seen, albeit briefly, one depot. We were about to cross another road with tram-tracks along it, said father. Meanwood Road this time, and route No.6.

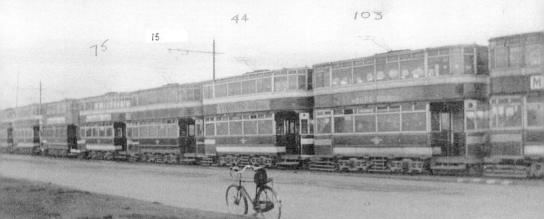

Plate 16: Part of the long line of tramcars on the single track siding at Low Fields Road for Elland Road Football Ground. Cars 75, 15, 44 and 103 are identified in 1943. Note the anti-blast netting on the windows and the author's bike. Author.

Further, then, up Shaw Lane to Headingley Lane where we turned right and alongside another line of tracks. This, I was told, was 1-Lawnswood route and hardly was that said than father said to watch out for Headingley' tram-sheds'. Well now, all of a sudden my tramway horizons had been advanced by the discovery of three new (to me) tram routes and two depots as well.

Would my parents and their two friends, whose car it was, like to become members of a tennis club in South or West Leeds? No, of course not, but I might have found more routes and more tram-sheds...!

On arrival at the tennis courts which were close by the Lawnswood terminus in Otley Road my parents would go 'on court', thus allowing me to go down to the fence/hedge bordering the road, where I could see the terminus which was in the roadway at the time. I could also watch the cars as they came from Leeds with 1-Lawnswood, via City Square up.

Then, as the cars came back from the terminus, their destination indicators told me further stories:-

Depot	*could be Headingley that we had just gone past.*
2-Moortown	*I didn't know for certain where that was.*
2 Circular	*Roundhay via Moortown - Ah, I remember seeing those come down from Street Lane past Canal Gardens when we had a day out at Roundhay Park. The cars always came down the middle track at Canal Gardens and we had to step out from the queue barriers in front of the No.4 cars to board them.*
3 Circular	*Roundhay via Harehills - I knew that blind very well! The word 'Roundhay' on the top line of the destination panel was scalloped on the underside in*

order to get the words 'via Harehills' in so that the
three words would be clearly visible. The words 'via
Sheepscar' or 'via City' or 'via City Square' were
shown in the narrower aperture at the base of the
indicator box.

City Square   *I had not been there yet but had heard a lot about it*
from father who worked in the Motor Taxation Office
at 5, South Parade, off Park Row, not far from City
Square.

My father and mother always tried to explain where places were and I began to recognise districts of Leeds when they were spoken about. When my father brought home the small timetable booklet (about 4" square) of Leeds trams and buses, reading became adventurous.

Sometime in 1936/37 as a result of chasings and scrappings between opposing groups of boys in Milan Road, my mother came out of the house in the back street and stopped myself and another boy arguing. She delivered a right bawling-out to both of us. As an immediate result we stopped arguing and shook hands. Thus Stuart Pickford and myself became friends and have remained so ever since. I was then 10 years old and Stuart was 12.

During the last 63 years we have ridden on trams, photographed trams and lectured on trams and very shortly after shaking hands we would be around together in Harehills after school-time. Stuart went to Harehills School on Roundhay Road and I went to the 'opposition', Gipton School on Harehills Road. Eventually Stuart went to Roundhay School whilst I went to the City of Leeds School.

Stuart's house was 25 and mine was 22 Milan Road nearer to Harehills Lane and so we were able to be near the No.9 route and indeed we were down on to Roundhay Road frequently. It was always helpful to compare observations and notes on the trams and, an excitement for me again, Stuart's father owned a motor car, a green Morris Oxford MU 7804 of 1934.

Also about this time both our families got their milk from Mr Pearson's dairy - premises on Harehills Road and their newspapers from Crotty's shop nearby. Both shops were near the No.11 terminus at Harehills Sorting Office. Thus visits to these shops gave us the opportunity to see the cars on the 9-Dewsbury Road route. Mr Pearson owned two green Model T Ford vans with registration numbers U-7xxx and many times we would beg a lift with him to his garage at the back of premises in Milan Street.

My school up to late 1938 was still Gipton Council School on

Harehills Road and my family's routine was fairly straight forward with the trams being part of the accepted daily routine. Everything about the trams interested me but I was never able really to know Leeds Tramways because we were unable to travel far sufficiently often to learn more. However, that difficulty was going to be overcome for me, though I did not know it at this time.

After 60 years I have tried to understand why Leeds trams, starting in this particular period of growing-up with the cars from 1933 to 1939, have always held such a fascination for me. I cannot really give a definitive answer to this question. It could have been the fascination of things that ran on rails and that these things were part of my 'big City' that I wanted to explore and get to know.

My mother's upbringing and training caused her to write and make notes about interesting and ordinary things. It is likely that she passed on this inherent interest and recording ability to me.

Recently I bought a copy of the video by Online Video and Leeds Transport Historical Society entitled 'Leeds Trams' in which there are views of cars during this period. The video made it very apparent to me that my parents and myself took the cars so much for granted, after all, the cars would never change and they would always be running in Leeds, wouldn't they?

In those days my parents could not have afforded to take many photographs, even though Mother had a camera which she used many a time before she was married. After 1925 to 1928 when the Pivotals were introduced to Leeds, most of the very old cars were scrapped - the ones that I never saw and those my mother would not have photographed.

The 'old cars' were given the letter 'A' after their number when new cars arrived in Leeds between 1926 and 1931. These details can be found in the 1969 publication 'A Fleet History of Leeds City Transport' by Leeds and District Transport News. The assistance of this valuable booklet is very much appreciated and acknowledged.

I knew nothing of the surprising number of 'A-cars', not necessarily in service all at one time but I must have seen and ridden on these 'old cars' as they travelled on the Harehills routes. They would be between 25 and 30 years old in 1939 - some of them would have been withdrawn from service and/or scrapped before I was able to have taken note. There were only eight 'A-cars' left when I discovered them in 1942 (plus three conversions!). (See 115A in Plate 18)

This perpetually futile worry about the fact that, up to a certain year pre-war, the 'old cars' were running and so was I (but with no recognition of these cars!) is totally historically frustrating.

Plate 17: Car 468 (ex-Hull) and Car 83 at 11-Harehills Road terminus in 1943. 468 is waiting for 83 to come back over the crossover at Harehills Post Sorting Office. Author.

It was not until 1940 after I had gathered up some knowledge of Leeds trams and when I first saw one of the London cars, 27x, that I realised that if there were any old cars left that had a number beginning with the 'magic two', then the numbers could only be between 280 and 299. Even in 1940 before the idea of starting the 'Book' occurred to me, I thought I knew about most of the cars numbered between 200 and the London's 27x.

In hindsight, the phrase 'the magic twos' did not enter my vocabulary until I found car 297 in Swinegate Depot. (Chapter 4). It was then that I realised that it would be most exciting to find any of the other remaining balcony cars whose numbers began with a 2. Cars of the same balcony type but whose numbers began with a 3 were accepted as normal service cars at Harehills and on cross-city journeys to school from 1940 onwards. I do not remember seeing or riding on any balcony cars whose numbers began with a 2. My use of the word 'magic' to refer to some of the old balcony tramcars in this book is not because of the supernatural quality of the cars, though to my young mind they could have been so, but because of the excitement I felt when I vaguely learnt for the first time about the existence of these tramcars. The knowledge that old tramcars still existed whose numbers began with a 2 and which I had never seen gave me a feeling about them that was mysteriously captivating with an almost enchanting quality. When I eventually found these remaining cars in 1942 they were enchanting.

Although a fair number of balcony cars of similar shape to those accepted cars whose number began with a 3, but whose number began with a ONE and had an A after the number, were still in service before the war I do not remember seeing, or expecting to see, an A after the number. This A and the reason for it was totally unknown to me before 1940. For instance I did not know until 1942 that car 118, an English Electric Pivotal and balcony car 118A, a car built at Kirkstall Works by Leeds Tramways about 1908, were both in service between 1926/27 and say, 1939. I was far too young...! etc.

Memory is a fickle thing. I do remember hearing vague statements about 'A-cars' from 1940 onwards, probably, but impossible now to confirm, as a result of travelling across Leeds to school and thus meeting people with a wider knowledge of Leeds 'happenings'.

These vague statements about 'A-cars' could only have referred to those balcony cars that remained in service and then were stored rather than scrapped at the beginning of the war.

Could these cars be my first 'secrets' to be discovered about Leeds trams? Statements about a 'separate set of numbered cars', however many there were, would be a 'secret' to me until I was older and could start my own investigations into their location, provided that

Plate 18: Car 115A, one of the 'A-cars' at Torre Road Top Shed in late 1944. Mr Bedell, Chief Draughtsman at Leeds City Transport, is on the step of 115A whilst Norman Kirk and the author are in the group on the left. See Plate 68. V.E. Burrows.

such cars had not been scrapped, war or not, before I obtained information about their whereabouts.

So I must have subconsciously taken note of the cars that I saw in the streets and, presumably, this is why so many hidden memories are being triggered and uncovered.

However, in 1931 when I was five years old the Horsfields (P.35s) were put into service and a quantity of old cars disappeared. This time the cars that the Horsfields replaced must have been numbered up to 254 and were likely to have been in service in Harehills up to 1931. Further, when the Middletons and 272, 273 and 274 arrived, more old cars with numbers beginning with the 'magic two' disappeared by 1935. Similarly with 277, 278 and 279 in 1940. What were 275 and 276?

Records will probably say when cars were taken out of service and scrapped prior to the war, but my little world and even father's 'intelligence network' would not have known about such things.

It is faintly possible that father and I could have found out about these 'statistics', had we known where to ask, through people father knew; but in those days that sort of 'investigation' was not only unheard-of, it would not have been allowed.

This is where I find myself 'kicking at the ghosts of opportunity' and saying to myself: 'If only...!!

The Leeds fleet of tramcars was fairly new from 1934/1935 to 1939 but very little was recorded by my family about this period of relative tramway stability and improvement in Leeds. Not much was recorded but many deep impressions were made.

Plate 19: Car 155 - the first Horsfield or P.35 to be built by Brush of Loughborough seen on the traverser at their works in 1931. Courtesy Brush, Loughborough.

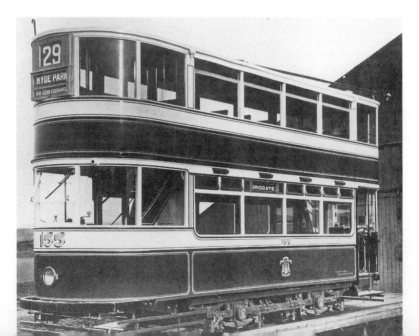

Chapter Two

'A Tram-mad Youngster ...'

One morning in December, 1938, my mother woke me up and said, 'How would you like to go to the City of Leeds School in the centre of Leeds?' That was not a question that a boy of twelve years could answer properly, having had no experience of anything other than at Gipton School. That the proposed school was of very good standard there was no doubt as my parents had done their homework very well. Apart from the idea of progressing to a good secondary school from a good primary one and perhaps thinking how much my parents would be paying for me to go to a good school, it soon occurred to me that this would be the first time that I would be able to travel to Leeds, or Town as we were now beginning to call it, on my own or perhaps with one or two other local boys.

Once it was decided that I was going to the City of Leeds School the next thing was to get the uniform (more expense for parents). The only place to buy School Uniforms was Rawcliffe's in Duncan Street, right next to the busiest tram junction in Leeds. Their card as suppliers to the City of Leeds School is shown here.

Fairly soon afterwards and just before Christmas, my mother and I went to Town, where we walked from the 'Barriers' the short distance down Briggate to the Boar Lane/Briggate/Duncan Street/Lower Briggate crossroads.

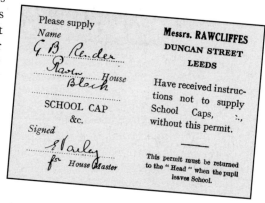

Plate 20: *The card issued to pupils of the City of Leeds School to authorise purchase of school uniforms from Rawcliffe's of Duncan Street. September 1939.* Author/Rawclifffe's.

We stopped at the curved pedestrian safety barrier on the footpath from Briggate into Duncan Street. Now, this was the very first time that I had been allowed to stand anywhere in Town for any reason, let alone to look and absorb traffic and trams. Even in December and in the cold, my mother agreed to let me watch all the activity at this busy place.

Plate 21: Boar Lane, Briggate junction about 1937. The barrier where mother and I stopped in December 1938 is hidden by the top deck of the top left-hand bus. Yorkshire Post.

What a place take in the sights and noises! A 'place in heaven' for a tram-mad youngster of 12 years of age!

Trams were going in all directions; routes 14, 16, 18, 19, 20 and 21 being new to me. I had heard about them but had not seen the actual destination blinds on cars in service.

There were Pivotals, P.35s, non-waterproof cars, cars from Beeston of various shapes. Oh boy! This was marvellous!

'Now here's an older-looking Pivotal (404 say) and an even older-looking car similar to a Pivotal but the wheel structure is different - the car is on 5-Beeston.

'Hey! down there, under the railway bridge in Lower Briggate, turning into another street, is a car in '272-blue' that seems to be a longer car than 272. Surely, that must be a Middleton car! The first one that I have seen. It's impossible to see the number at this distance - no good worrying about whether it's 255 or not.

'Now, what's this coming down Briggate on 4-Kirkstall? 348

looking very clean and smart; perhaps it's just been painted? It looks like an older car, perhaps one of the 'non-waterproof' cars with new top-ends. The bottom deck looks very much like those of the 'non-waterproof' cars. Look where the destination indicator box is on 348. It looks as though we should be able to see-out-front all round upstairs. A bit like a 272, maybe? Let's compare 348's lower-deck front windows and panels with those of 33x coming along Boar Lane, Yes, it is similar so 348 looks like it used to be an 'empty-top-end' car, We must have a ride on one of those cars. 348 is on '4' so it will have come from Harehills. We must watch out for one of these cars on our visits to town.

Secret thought: 'I shall be up and down to town twice a day soon - bags of chances to ride on one of 348's type, I hope!'

'But wait a minute, coming up Lower Briggate to the stop at Dyson's is another car on 6-Meanwood but, although similar to 348, it looks different somehow. The car is passing me into Duncan Street and I am trying to fathom what is different. The car is 367 and is past before I can decide what makes it different to 348. Mark that down in the 'learning of the trams!' Because 367 has come from south of

Map 1 - Boar Lane/Briggate Junction and surrounding area in 1933. By kind permission of the Ordnance Survey, Southampton.

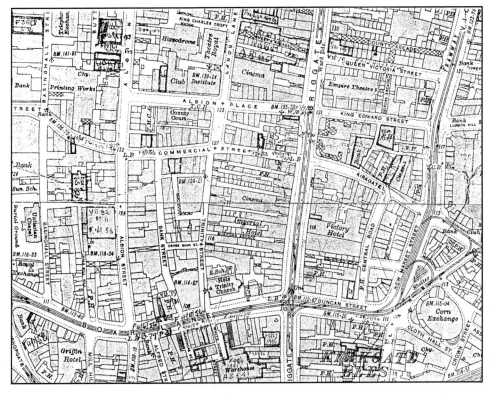

Leeds it may have equipment to enable it to go on Beeston Hill.' (Even then I had heard about the Beeston route and that only cars with special brakes could go there). 'I wonder how many cars are like 348 and how many are like 367, which has a white band on the side below the windows on the top deck. 348 has gone along Boar Lane, now out of my sight. Did that car have a white band like 367? I didn't notice!

Plate 22: *The Coat of Arms of the City of Leeds School on the front of an invitation to the School Sports Day at West Park, on 19 July 1939.* Author.

'And now here is a 'non-waterproof' car, 33x, with no route number box, coming along Boar Lane painted blue where 367 had a white band.' I noticed that the 'non-waterproof' cars usually had a white (or cream) band like 367 and also were white or cream just above the wheels. 'There are too many differences between these cars. It's going to be a difficult job to get to 'know' all the cars. Obviously I am intending to do just that. What is the highest car number I have seen so far? 426, on Lawnswood, which is a Pivotal but even this car is in some way different from 84 behind it on 4-

Plate 23: *Car 228 in Vicar Lane on 26 May 1939. The sticker on the car's fender read 'Tulip Time at Temple Newsam'.* H.B. Priestley/National Tramway Museum Collection.

Hawksworth Road and there is a difference too between the third car in the line at the Barriers, 46, with 'Briggate' up and both 426 and 84. I wonder what the top number is and what sort of car will that be? 'Coming along Boar Lane now is a P.35. Smooth cars these! Totally different to the familiar Pivotal shape. 173 is on 2 circular - Roundhay via Moortown. Looking the other way along Duncan Street, here's a car on 9-Dewsbury Road - 144 which is turning down Lower Briggate. Car 46 is going back up Briggate across a crossover at my end of the Barriers and I can tell again that there is a difference between the two cars 46 and 144. The roof is different somehow. I had disappeared into a world of trams and Mother, with an exasperatedly tolerant 'Come on now!' brought me back to our reality because we had to get to Rawcliffe's.

We were both very cold. I hadn't noticed this in the excitement, but Mother had and so we walked along into the warmth of Rawcliffe's.

Trams were not the only vehicles at that cross-roads. There were Leeds buses, other red buses with doors in the middle instead of the back, motor cars, cyclists, vans and lots of people, all going somewhere, but I only saw the trams... !

The badge for the new school was the Leeds Coat of Arms with the motto 'Non Sine Pulvere Palma' and that was on the cap on the front panel which had a triangular black panel on either side, signifying that my School House was to be Raven House. The cap was blue, the same as the blazer which had the Coat of Arms on the pocket, which I was very proud to wear. All the trams had the Coat of Arms on their 'uniforms' too!

We were out of Rawcliffe's in quicksticks because we could see and hear trams going past the shops whilst we were being served and I didn't want to miss anything having been presented with such an opportunity for tramcar observation. Mother agreed, under a fair amount of pressure from me, to turn left out of Rawcliffe's and actually walk to Corn Exchange: another 'first-time' event for me.

We turned the corner from Duncan Street into New Market Street. (See Map 1 p. 35) The word 'corner' is somewhat academic as the whole area is spacious over to the Corn Exchange building. We walked a little further to the junction with Kirkgate and stood for a moment or two there. There was too much 'tram and tracks' to take in at one go, especially for the second time on a cold December day. My mother felt the cold but I was too occupied to notice a little thing like cold weather! So, reluctantly we walked through Kirkgate to Briggate Barriers. The 'top' barrier had cars for Chapeltown and

Plate 24: Car 400 in the depths of wartime in 1942 at the Clock Cinema terminus of the 3-Harehills route. The photograph shows how dull the trams became due to wartime restrictions. The driver and conductress were well-known, but not their names. Author.

Moortown. We had to go to the barrier nearest Boar Lane to get on a No.3 Harehills car at the driver's end. We gradually warmed up on the journey home. I had seen lots and lots of cars of all sorts today, but there was no sign of 400 anywhere.

We got off the car at Shepherds Lane stop, adjacent to Harehills School, not Harehills Corner, and walked up Lascelles Terrace to Harehills Road, crossed over the road and up Milan Road home. What a day of tramcar discovery! I thought, 'when will my parents allow me to look at trams in such a location again?'

I do not remember details but Christmas 1938 and New Year 1939 must have been quite exciting. I had just left the security of Gipton School and was about to start on an adventure at a brand-new school and, I hoped, on all manner of adventures with Leeds trams.

Chapter Three

NEW SCHOOLS, WARTIME AND THE 'BOOK'

A nd so it came about that on January 11th 1939, all togged up in new cap and blazer and raincoat with the Leeds Coat of Arms on the blazer pocket, I was allowed and obliged to travel on the trams, alone for the first time, from Harehills to Town where I got off the car at the Grand Theatre stop in New Briggate, then walked up Merrion Street to the school in Woodhouse Lane, opposite Rowland Winn's Garage. Mr F.R. Worts was the Headmaster. Whoever sited the City of Leeds School in Woodhouse Lane must have been very forward thinking because there were no tram routes anywhere near the building or school-yard. Probably as well for me, otherwise I should have been listening for the cars going past instead of concentrating on Latin verbs or the Po delta or other such interesting subjects!

On the journey home from school (never mind the school-time) it was necessary to walk down to the tram stop at Lewis's opposite the Paramount Picture House to wait for a No.3 coming up Briggate from the barriers. At this time of the day, 4.00pm in January, all the lights were on, shops lit up, Briggate looked exciting, even the sweet shop near to the Paramount looked inviting, but I only had the tram fare home - one penny!

Alighting from the car at Harehills Corner instead of Shepherds Lane was always so much more interesting. There were more trams to see and take mental note of and I was able to examine Mr Frew's shop to see if there was anything new or different in the shop window. Hornby 'Dublo' had recently made its debut, a highly practical gauge of railway models. No lingering here though, Mother would be anxious for me to be home.

I never had any need to get off any car at Sheepscar, but for some reason the fare from either Town or Harehills to Sheepscar remains in memory. It was one half penny (school or child's fare). The tram tickets were fairly substantial documents and

Plate 25: Two tickets of two old pence each for the tram fare from Harehills to City Square on 11 January 1945. Author.

the two I still have from January 11th 1945 were printed by the Glasgow Numerical Printing Co. and were for the adult fare - twopence, from Harehills to City Square on the day of my call-up into the Regiment. In passing, the tram tickets were of different colours for different values. I remember that the threepenny tickets were brown! What that meant to me was that it wasn't until I left school and obviously was not a 'child' or 'school' fare any longer, that I would ever get a brown ticket and I would have to be travelling a long way for that fare. In 1939, I could not imagine where I could go for threepence!

However, I was at a new school, had a new uniform, found new friends and a new freedom. Apart from schoolwork, homework and similar essentials, there were plenty of opportunities to see trams and eventually, because one of the subjects at school was drawing (engineering, not art) I found that I was able to draw out, from memory, side views of the Horsfield cars, thus learning more about the 'face' of construction of these cars.

I remember nothing about the first day of travel to the new school, apart from directions from parents on how to get there, but when travelling on the cars later it became an absolute necessity to sit at the front upstairs or in a similar position at the rear of the cars, especially if the car was a Pivotal or one like, say, 404.

On the Pivotal cars, to give them their full name for once, when I sat upstairs on the curved seat on the left hand side of the destination indicator box (some with KELBUS handles) I could not only see-out-front very well, but if I twisted round and looked over the brass stair handrails (see Plate 12), there was the driver in 'plan-view' and I could watch how he operated the controller. That is, of course, if the driver had not put the flaps down. To try and understand the driver's actions, to watch him over the hand-rails caused a great deal of body twisting. Because I could not drive any kind of vehicle and therefore did not have 'road-sense', all I could do was to try and remember what the driver did in readiness for the time that I would be lucky enough to drive. There was no doubt in my mind that I would be able to drive trams, one day! If the car was 404 or similar (or like 399 at Crich, now) the seat position as just described was wooden and straight and was formed from the vertical wood/glass partition and door that sealed off the driver and his open platform from upstairs passengers, thus stopping cold blasts of air coming up from the outside. The door stopped me watching the driver too. There was no necessity for flaps on this type of car.

In lieu of this partition the Pivotals made by Brush and English Electric and some of the cars made by Leeds City Tramways had folding, black, wooden, heavy flaps which the driver would clatter down from the vertically-held position to a horizontal position, thus providing a form of anti-cold-draught-up-the-stairs from the driver's platform. These flaps were positioned at the top of the stairs and were shaped to fit the stairwell.

At Briggate Barriers where front-loading was normal, these black flaps were put up into the vertical position by the driver. They were always put down with a wallop before the tram set off. At some stops, when the conductor was collecting fares upstairs and could not (or would not) get back downstairs to pull the bell-cord for right-away, he would go to the front of the car, open the nearside window that would open (the other one said it wouldn't!) and, when everyone was 'on' the car, he would STAMP twice on these flaps.

The 'stamp-stamp' never failed to make us jump in spite of our being used to it. I wondered many a time if the driver jumped too! On the Horsfields we sat on the off-side-front of the cars, upstairs, facing the door and stair-partition, with heads screwed round 90 degrees to the right to see-out-front, as on 180 at Crich now. Of course, if one was lucky enough to ride on 272, or even one of the converted cars like 348 or 367, then we faced forward, comfortably, with no destination indicator box to impede forward vision. It was about now - mid 1939 - that I began to note down tramcar numbers, their type and all manner of other details, 'as observed'. I also tried to mentally 'photograph' the cars so I could begin to 'tell' them without seeing the number. A tram-car 'gricer', I suppose, but that

Plate 26: The upstairs front seats of Horsfield 180 at Crich on 28 November 1995.
Author.

Plate 27: The juntion of Harehills Road, Ashley Road, Stanley Road and Beckett Street in 1942. Leeds Local and Family History Library.

obnoxious word 'gricer' wasn't invented then, at least, it wasn't in my world. It was not until late 1941 did I start the 'Book'. It had taken a long time for me to find out how many Pivotal cars there were but by 1941 I had learnt that the Brush Company at Loughborough had built 75 cars (Nos. 1 - 75), the English Electric Company at Preston had built a further 75 cars (Nos. 76 - 150) and Leeds City Transport had built 36 cars at Kirkstall Works. Thus there were 186 Pivotals in service in Leeds, many of them seen in the Harehills area. On journeys to school, cars on other routes were noted as I saw them, but I still did not know much about these routes, particularly Sheepscar to Chapeltown and Moortown, also Sheepscar (Golden Cross) to Meanwood, even though I'd heard from Mother that cars used to go up Meanwood Road and turn left up Woodhouse Street to Hyde Park and beyond. The street-map that showed this old route

Plate 28: The same junction as Plate 27, fifty years later in 1992. Author.

was all very well, but I hadn't seen this area of Leeds yet.

Cars coming out of Meanwood Road had 8-Elland Road up, another unknown place. If father had wanted to go he might have taken me to the Leeds United Football Ground at Elland Road. Then look at the 'fleets' of trams that I would have seen All the 'old cars' were used as Football Specials. It doesn't do to dream.

Some cars on Meanwood were like 348 (or 367?) similar to the ones I had seen that Saturday at Boar Lane/Briggate Junction. Not quite like 348, but perhaps like 367, there was something more 'stable' about those cars on Meanwood. They didn't 'bounce' on joints like 348 so I must find out the difference.

Later that year experience showed me that most of the cars on Meanwood and Elland Road routes were generally those which I referred to as 'Beeston cars' i.e. 370-393, 399 and 402 (except 389) plus the Converts, as I learnt to call them. The Converts that ran on Beeston were various numbers between 332 and 369, but I had not seen all these cars yet. There was still a lot to learn, All the Beeston cars of whatever type had brakes and equipment to enable them to be safe on Beeston Hill, obviously. Perhaps I would be lucky and see a Beeston Convert like 347 next to a non-Beeston Convert like 348 and then I could compare the cars. Perhaps if I asked the drivers, they might explain the difference?

If these cars were equipped for Beeston, why were these the usual cars on Meanwood and Elland Road? I knew they could go anywhere on the system but why were the Pivotals or 'non-Beeston Converts' not on Meanwood or Elland Road? They were both fairly level routes. A question answered in later years when I found that they only had hand brakes.

Since that December day in 1938 when Mother and I stood at Boar Lane/ Briggate Junction, a thought kept pushing itself to the forefront of my daily existence. All the trams running about Leeds during the day, where are the cars kept at night? I had seen where Chapeltown and Headingley Depots were, but there must be more than those two to cater for the numbers of cars that I regularly saw on my way to school. I must find out one day even if it means Stuart Pickford and myself riding all the routes. But, of course, we wouldn't have been allowed to do that, apart from the cost. I must be patient.

Another thought comes to mind. My family never went to town by bus! There were buses at Harehills Corner from Dib Lane, Foundry Lane and Gledhow, but they all went to the so-called Central Bus Station which was nowhere near Briggate and the shops and certainly not near Woodhouse Lane, even the bottom end. In addition the bus routes went through areas that were completely strange to us so we always went to Town by tram.

Come to think of it, we never went to Town on the nearest tram route to Milan Road, i.e. the one at the bottom of Milan Road, 9-Dewsbury Road. This route went to the Corn Exchange and we never went there. I wish I'd known why not!

One direct 'tram' result of going to the City of Leeds School was that I found my third depot and it wasn't very far away from my own home, surprisingly enough. A friend made at the new school lived at the Police Station at the junction of Ashley Road/Harehills Road/Stanley Road where his father was Superintendent. I remember going along Ashton Road and down Ashley Road on a Saturday morning and being able to look over the wall of the Police Station yard and watch the cars coming into Stanley Road Depot presumably off 'early turn'. Later on they would begin to go out on service for Saturday afternoon/evening duties. A grandstand view of a bit of the old world of Leeds Tramways. Three depots found now. How many more are there?

Mr W.A. Camwell's classic photograph of the seven Pivotals outside Stanley Road Depot epitomises my 'world of tramcars' (Plate 29). Once I discovered this depot, it became a magnet for me. There were tracks and tracks, all off one single line in Stanley Road. There was nearly always some movement of cars, either within the depot or just outside it. Even with some of the tall doors closed, to look inside, 'round the doors' and see all the cars in lines on each track except No.7, was thoroughly exciting.

Another photograph exactly a year later on, 26 May 1939, by H.B. Priestley and received by courtesy of Mrs Rosemary Thacker, the Librarian at the National Tramway Museum at Crich, shows the inside of Stanley Road Depot and must have been taken about the same time as I first discovered the depot. What is so interesting about this view is that on Track 7 there appears to be a works car with snow-plough board attached, which looks as though it may have been a British Thomson-Houston car of 1899 which was cut down when taken out of service. If so it could have been one of the cars I might have seen but could not remember, before the Horsfields arrived in Leeds in 1931. I cannot remember seeing any works cars in Stanley Road Depot, but if this car was there when I looked over the Police Station wall and on subsequent visits to the front of the 'tram sheds', there is a very tenuous connection between myself and the cars that I might have seen or understood before 1931. That possibility is a very, very deep down bit of tramway history, partially interesting,

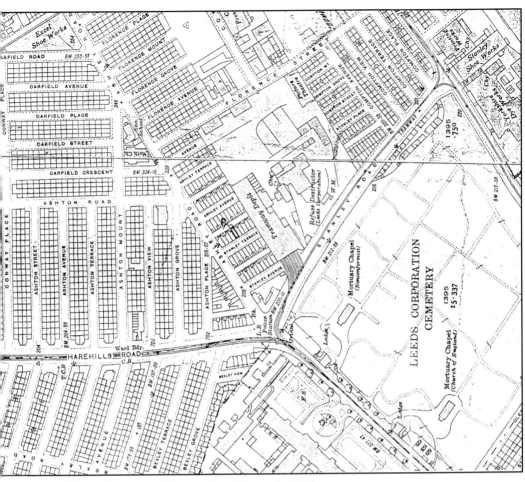

Map 2: Location of Stanley Road Depot in 1933

Map 3: Harehills Road, Roundhay Road with Gipton School, 1933.

By kind permission of Ordnance Survey, Southampton.

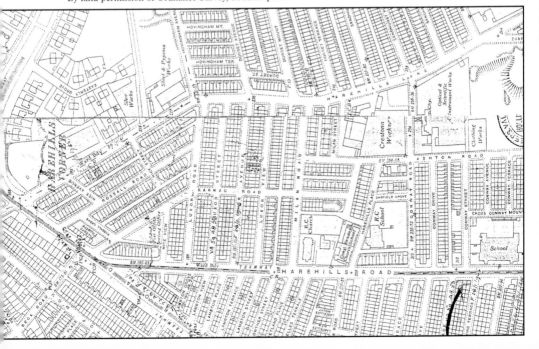

Plate 29: A symphony of tramcars. The classic depot photograph of seven Pivotal cars, specially posed at Stanley Road Depot on 26 May 1938. See Plate 48. W.A. Camwell/National Tramway Museum Collection.

partially historically-infuriating again.

Whilst referring to 'tram sheds' I am reminded of two terms or phrases used by my family then (1939) and were taken for granted as well as the trams:

> 1. *'Leeds Tramways'. Whatever the proper name was for the 'Department', i.e. 'Leeds City Tramways and Transport Department' or 'Leeds City Transport Department', we always referred to the 'body' that operated the cars as 'Leeds Tramways' and I still do!*
> 2. *Stanley Road Depot was known locally as 'the tram sheds'. I learnt this after I had found them and when, in 1940, we were passing them every day. I think my parents used the word 'tram sheds' in connection with any depot in Leeds. I assume that railways had 'engine sheds' as an accepted type of building and so the buildings fulfilling the same purpose for trams were similarly described. We did not, however, refer to the trams in the depot as being 'on shed' as in railway parlance.*

Later on in 1939, although everybody had Hitler and the Nazis in Germany in mind, even us, as youngsters, began to understand that these people were going to cause a great deal of trouble in the world outside Leeds. Searchlights could already be seen practising aircraft 'coning'.

This was confirmed at the City of Leeds School when we were all told that if war was declared then the whole school would be evacuated to a 'safer area' as air raids on cities would begin. What would happen to the trams, I thought? Sure enough, after I had been at the new school for only two terms and was just settling down, the school was evacuated and we all went to Lincoln in September, 1939. Apart from Hitler and Co., Lincoln was where I found my first girl friend - on the No.6 bus from Lincoln to Swanpool (we were 13 years old). 'Once bitten, forever smitten' as the advertisement said.

The fairly short period of evacuation opened my eyes to the world outside Harehills and No.3 trams, but the tramcar 'world' inside Leeds was still going to be exciting, war or no war. In the so-called safer area of Lincoln, Nazi planes used to come over the airfields of Lincolnshire and bomb them and they even flew down Lincoln High Street strafing the place. We were returned to Leeds in January 1940 to find that the City of Leeds School would be closing down (we had no idea why) and that we would have to find another school to go to. As fees were payable per term in those days, my parents had to place me in a school that they could afford. Roundhay School fees were six guineas per term which was too expensive and so, at three guineas per term, Cockburn High School, off Dewsbury Road, right across Leeds, was decided upon.

Well now, two schools in one year and this one was miles away from home in an area none of us knew and we were obviously going to have to start studies all over again. However, never mind wartime or the blackout or air raid sirens or another school, my little world was enlarging rapidly and now an opportunity had arisen for me to learn more about Leeds and where the tram routes went that I had no idea about. But, exciting though this new school and travel would be, the idea of travelling all that way to school from Harehills was unheard of for us in those days. The distance was about three to four miles, not on any minor ring roads or similar. There were no roads like that in that direction and there were few motor cars anyway, there was no petrol for them. There was a war on, you know!

Those three or four miles would be undertaken 'on the tram', in the blackout, the cars stopping every 300 yards or so at request stops, fare stages and 'robots' (traffic lights), thus taking about 35 minutes for the journey. All these conditions were accepted as normal at the time and there would be four of us travelling together so our parents were a little easier in their minds about our having to be away on our own for so long and so far away.

On the positive side the journey to school and back would be on a tram route that I didn't know and there would be umpteen other routes joining or crossing ours, also unknown to me. Never mind

Plate 30: Inside Stanley Road Depot on 26 May 1939, exactly one year after W.A. Camwell's visit. Hidden away at the back of Track 7 (right) can be seen Snowplough 12. See Plate 31. H.B. Priestley/National Tramway Museum Collection.

school, these journeys were going to be exciting, notwithstanding homework and other school matters.

My parents worked it out that I could go to school two ways. First, I could get on the No.9-Dewsbury Road tram at the Congregational Church in Harehills Road and travel across Leeds for one penny (school fare), get off the car at Moor Road and walk to school. Secondly, I could get on a car at Harehills Corner going to either Briggate or Corn Exchange and change cars at either place. The car fare on this route cost one penny (school) from Harehills to Town

Plate 31: Snowplough 12 outside Stanley Road Depot on 26 May 1938. W.A. Camwell/National Tramway Museum Collection.

and one penny from Town to Dewsbury Road. This second route was discarded because it would have cost my parents four pence per day as against two pence per day on the No.9. Thoughts! Wasn't Moor Road on the No.12-Middleton Route where 255 was? So, in January 1940 it was necessary for me to have another new uniform, i.e. a school cap in brown and gold with CHS on the front instead of the Leeds Coat of Arms. It was also necessary to go down to Rawcliffe's again and we were able to stand at the same barrier at Boar Lane/Briggate crossroads to absorb again all the tram activities there, exactly one year since our last visit.

There was a war on now, albeit 'phoney' and things were different. Where and when had all the headlamp masks been made and fitted? There was white paint all over the place to assist or to be seen in the blackout. Inside the cars all lamps/bulbs had a mask over them. As I remember, the Pivotals and cars that had similar light fittings had a small cylinder with a thin slot in the base, fitted in the manner of a proper shade which would only allow a very small amount of light through. I cannot remember when anti-blast netting was put on the windows. Whenever it was, the netting with small peepholes was horrible stuff and made the car miserable inside.

Then, almost with a double-take, I happened to look up to the trolley-poles. There were no trolley-poles! All the cars that I could see had a 'wire-thing' on the roof that was pressing up to the 'tram-wires'. In this lay-man's language I realised that all the trolley-booms and wheels had gone and, when I looked down where the bamboo poles once were, they had gone too! I had not noticed this major change on the trams. Probably because the trolley-booms were not at my eye-level and in any case the trolley-booms were such an accepted part of the cars that they would hardly be expected to change. Mark

Plate 32: A complete model of Stanley Road Depot on 8 April 1998. John Baxter Photography.

it down, that lad! Always look at everything!

So what was the new 'trolley' that the cars now had? Whatever it was called, the reversing of the trolley appeared to be a much easier performance than the routine I had watched at Harehills Road Terminus. My mother, who hadn't known about this new trolley either, and I saw a car come down Briggate with 'Briggate' up and stop just past the Boar Lane end of the Barriers crossover.

The conductor changed the destination and number to '2-Chapeltown', the driver secured the brake handle on the ratchet and took the reversing lever and point iron and schedule board to the other end of the car, where he applied the hand-brake as the conductor released the hand-brake at his end. The conductor put the ring chain over his brake handle. The conductor then stepped round the back of the car on the rear fender and unhooked the 'trolley' rope ring from its hook on the windscreen upright and stepped down onto the roadway, holding the rope. 'What does the rope do?' we thought as we watched this procedure. The driver moved the car slowly towards the Barriers over the crossover and as he did so the conductor pulled hard on the rope, with both hands, and the new 'trolley' was pulled into the reverse direction, i.e. a trailing direction. Because the conductor pulled hard on the rope, the 'trolley' lost contact with the overhead wire for a moment and the car stopped. The driver would realise that the trolley was changed over, and would wait for the conductor to release the rope upwards to contact the wire again and to put the rope ring back on its hook and to pull two rings on the bell-cord so that the driver could take his car to the far barrier to load up.

This change-over of trolley took a far shorter time to carry out than it has taken to write the activity and there was no fear of tripping or slipping with a long bamboo pole in hands. Just imagine how easy that procedure would be in the blackout. Now, even to my young mind, there must have been a tremendous amount of rearrangement of the overhead wires throughout the city to cater for the change-over. We had not seen any of the derricks doing anything on the overhead to make us ask questions about the new 'trolleys'.

The wheel at the end of the trolley boom had been replaced by a flat plate, but as neither Mother nor I had any mechanical knowledge then, we had to use our 'noddles' to work these things out. My mother said to me, 'I know who can tell us about this new trolley' and took me over to the Barriers' Office and found Inspector Crossley, whom she knew and asked him what the new trolleys were. Mr Crossley explained that the General Manager, Mr W. Vane Morland

Plate 33: Car 230, a Horsfield or P.35, at 11-Harehills Road Terminus in early 1943. The car is painted in wartime khaki with white paint, headlamp masks and anti-blast netting. See Plate 35. Author.

had decided to change over to the 'Bow-Collector'. So now we knew! The trolley changeover wasn't as simple as that of course. Much to our surprise we were also told that the change-over had been completed over a year previously and we hadn't noticed.

Incidentally, two other Inspectors often seen at Briggate Barriers were Inspector Joe Henry, whom father knew, and Inspector Brogden. Joe Henry's son worked in the Traffic Department at the Head Office in Swinegate.

Another addition to some of the cars and which I did notice was a wide, white band of paint applied to the dash under the headlamp, but above the number, at both ends to reflect a little in blackout driving. The Horsfields and Middletons, 272, 273 and 274 and the London cars 277-279 already had a cream strip at their fronts as part of their design and thus seemed not to require any painted additions.

Plate 34: Car 248, a Horsfield or P.35 at the Clock Cinema, Easterly Road, in 1943. The car is painted in the standard blue and cream but nevertheless with white fenders, headlamp masks and anti-blast netting. Author.

Plate 35: Cars 331, 230 and 22 in Duncan Street about 1936. Yorkshire Post.

As I was listening to Inspector Crossley telling us about the bow collector displacing the trolley boom, the last thing in my mind would have been cats' names! Surely there is no connection! There is, because forty six years later in Wales a ginger and white kitten was given to me and, of course, he had to be trained and named. I had no difficulty in naming him 'TROLI', mainly after Leeds trams, but partially after the Trolls in Norway.

Further to this in 1992 a black cat which was obviously homeless, had taken to visiting my house and sometimes stayed overnight if I let him. Very soon it became obvious that he wanted to stay with Troli and myself. So, he needed a name, and what more appropriate than another name from Leeds trams. I had Troli and 'BOOM' with me then and if ever a third cat had arrived I would have had Troli, Boom and 'WHEEL'. What a shame I couldn't have had a whole tramcar as well.

To return to the story. I have never referred to 272, 273 and 274 as 'Lance Corporals'! I consider they were too dignified to have that rank. In any case, you couldn't have a 'Lance-anything' on Lawnswood, could you?

Likewise through the years I have never referred to 151-254 as 'Showboats'. Always P.35's or Horsfields, or preferably just the number, 180 for instance. That was quite good enough for such capable cars! Pivotal cars were always Pivs. and were accepted as almost universal travellers except for Beeston, Middleton and Stanningley routes. Could they not have gone on Meanwood and Elland Road?

However, back to Boar Lane/Briggate Junction in 1940 where the cold weather sent us into Rawcliffe's again. Only a school cap this time because my parents thought a blazer for this school wasn't worth it. Duncan Street activities beckoned where Mother was persuaded to walk to New Market Street for me to look at things happening at Corn Exchange again. Then I discovered the markets and that side of Kirkgate, albeit from the Briggate side of New Market Street. There was obviously a very interesting track layout round here and, as Mother said, 'You will be riding all over that when you travel to the new school, so be patient, again.'

Another thing I noticed near the Corn Exchange building was the sharp-radius, part circle of track where the 14-Stanningley cars turned round. Also inside this semicircle of track were red double-decker buses with their doors in the centre of the bus. Surely they can't be Leeds buses, all our buses are blue. More and more to find out about.

All this tram activity at Corn Exchange was time-absorbing and I wondered where all the cars went, as was said in the Will Hay film

'The Ghost Train'. 'Where do 'ee come from? Where do 'ee go?'

What had I missed through not going to Corn Exchange? Patience or not, I knew that very shortly I would be passing Corn Exchange twice every day and would have plenty of time to find out about what went where, where the depots were and, most importantly to me, where 255 was.

In addition to all this, there was a whisper, so my father's intelligence network had told him, that Leeds Tramways had bought three tramcars from London, of all places. Fancy, that was unheard of, tramcars being transferred from one city to another. Certainly it was to happen to buses the other way round in 1941 when some Leeds buses were sent to London to replace London's buses destroyed in the blitz. But trams! My my! Then I wondered whether the London cars had arrived, when I would see the first one, what numbers would they have and what would they look like? I have learnt since that at the time Mother and I were standing in New Market Street, two of these London cars were actually in service but apparently on 25-Hunslet.

Now here was another case of not going to a particular part of Leeds. We would not normally have had any reason to be in Swinegate or Neville Street or, for that matter anywhere below (south of) Boar Lane. I had never heard of those streets although very shortly my journey to the new school would take me past some of these places. At the time of our being in New Market Street, Swinegate might just as well have been in London, for all I knew about it.

The change from the City of Leeds School to Cockburn High School took place at the worst time of the year weatherwise. The blackout was strictly enforced and on school-days in the early morning when I was about to leave home the blackout curtain was pulled aside, the hall light had to be off and inner doors closed before I went out of the house so that no light showed outside. This was about 8.00am and I walked up Ashton Road to turn right down to the bottom of Harehills Place where we waited for the car to come up one stop-length from the terminus at Harehills Sorting Office. I met up here with two other boys also going to Cockburn High School.

Although the sky was getting 'dawnish' it still felt like night. Imagine going on a 35 minute tramway journey at night in complete darkness - no lights anywhere in a totally strange area. How completely opposite were the circumstances, in comparison to the recent excitement pre-war, of a trip to Town to the theatre and the whole town brightly lit.

I remember hoping that the car down at the terminus would be a

Pivotal or other 'water-proof' car, but it very rarely was. I could sometimes hear the type of car as it set off from the Sorting Office and invariably at that time of the day the car was of the 'empty-top-end' (balcony) type - 318, say. After a week or two, experience and observations showed that Leeds Tramways always used these older cars at that time of day on these routes through tightly-packed housing areas like Beckett Street, Nippet Lane and Stoney Rock Lane. Notwithstanding any Nazi activities - Leeds had escaped these so far - we still had to go to school in snow, rain, slush or on frozen roads. No matter what the circumstances, the cars always got through, short of a derailment or an overhead power failure, which were rare events in our little world.

I can well remember the 'feel' of wintry weather as we waited at the bottom of Harehills Place. There was almost no traffic other than the trams and the only wheel-tracks in the snow were the tram rails, black parallel lines in a white Harehills Road. The white snow reflected what little dawn light there was and between the black rails the snow had been smoothed down by either the trams' lifeguards or trays acting as a snowplough 'to give the wheels a chance'.

Harehills Road is a wide road and normal sound in dry weather would be open and noise would 'bounce about' the area with no restriction. At that tram-stop at 8 o'clock on a January morning in 1940, snow on the ground and more coming down, everybody was muffled up against the cold, standing in silence, surrounded by silence, and resigned to a cold tram ride. (See Map 3, p. 45)

Car 318, say, would reluctantly set off from the Sorting Office and even the car would appear to muffle its way up the slope to our stop. The car's headlight was only a narrow slit in the headlamp mask and the masked lamps inside and upstairs only gave a downward glimmer, just enough to read a paper by if you got the paper in the right position which was impossible if the car was fairly full and the only seats left were on the aisle-side, upstairs of course. As for comparing homework notes - well!

Three other ex-City of Leeds School boys got on the car further along Harehills Road and we always assumed that the car would be going 'right through' to Dewsbury Road. We couldn't always make out the destination blind in the darkness or snow or both, but sometimes, explained by an official phrase like 'due to exigencies of the service', the car would stop at Kirkgate. All cars had to stop there anyway, not because of a compulsory stop, but because there were so many other cars in front. The conductor on our car would shout, 'All change please to the car behind. This car is going out of service'.

So the frozen or chilled passengers, having partially warmed up the car's top saloon were uprooted and there was a 'shuffling scrat-round' out on to the balcony where the seats were wet and empty or had snow on them, slither down the reverse stairs, off the conductor's platform, down the big step to the roadway and turn left along the side of 329, say, which was drawn up fender to fender to our car.

As we climbed aboard 329 the platform was very wet from snowy feet and if I got on the car on the right hand side of the centre grab-rail I could smear my hand on the controller handle and top with the raised name and notches - Dick, Kerr very often. Having carried out this purely personal little action I found that in so doing I had lost my place in the line of transferring passengers going upstairs and possibly the chance of a seat, but I would still have done it because it was my way at the time of getting to know the cars.

Back across the platform to the reverse stairs and up to the equally wet and empty top-end. Opening the saloon door - it slid to one side - Phew! The atmosphere was dense, smoke up to the ceiling and dampness on the floor. This car had come from Compton Road (Route 10) and was also going to Dewsbury Road and equally as full and dingy as our 318. The only seats I could find now were aisle-seats and on these I couldn't even look outside, even if it had been light enough. The windows were steamed up anyway. No wonder Leeds Tramways put these old cars on these routes in the early mornings. No sentimentality here! They couldn't have nice cars being 'soaked and smoked' like 318 and 329, could they! Sometimes I would go inside and try to sit next to the driver's platform window to see-out-front in the early morning. This wasn't always possible because it was too dark and in any case schoolboys at that time would have to give up their seats to a lady if required. We were shouted at by the conductor if we didn't. If I stood up next to the driver's door and held on to the straps hanging from the bell-cord tube, I couldn't see-out-front at all because the driver always had the long blind down on the door window behind him so that no reflections would affect his driving in the blackout. Later on in the year on the same type of balcony car and when it was daylight earlier and weather conditions easier, I was able to see-out-front and watch everything. More often than not, 318, say, would go right through to Dewsbury Road and we would be able to compare homework notes.

And still Leeds trams fascinated me!

It was quite an experience going past Stanley Road for the first few times when we could see out of the windows in drier weather. Into Beckett Street and into and out of loops on the single track, realising that the loops were controlled by little white lights on the overhead poles at each end of the loop, past St. James's Hospital down to where the cars from Compton Road came in. Then to York Road and the massive Quarry Hill Flats and possibly down Marsh Lane, but more often down New York Street past the new Central Bus Station that wasn't central at all.

The last paragraph was my impression of a ride to Town on one of the first journeys to my new school. After the worry and the novelty of the first few journeys, I settled down to take note of anything 'tramway' on the whole run.

Apart from the excitement of travelling over routes that I had never been on and the idea that school was at the end of the journey from Harehills, on subsequent journeys in clear weather I was looking out for tracks that branched off, or came into, or crossed the No.9 route. This is where a Pivotal was preferred to the 'empty-top-end' cars. At least I could sit at the front or back ends in the dry and look out for other tracks. The balcony cars, the proper name for 'empty-top-end' cars were usually too cold or steamed-up to try to see much out of them and the application of anti-blast netting limited vision tremendously. From Stanley Road towards Town there were five loops in Beckett Street, those I remember were at St. James's Hospital, another at Granville Street, another just before Nippet Lane. I always watched the effect of the control exercised by the pole-mounted white lights, although I cannot now remember the sequence.

By now I had observed tramcar numbers and types and so, on all journeys, lots of car details were noted. What type of controllers, were they the same at both ends? What sort of brakes did the various handles operate? How did the driver operate the points without using the point iron? Why did the driver throw-off and feed up again immediately when there was nothing visible on the road to cause such action? Were we getting to be 'top-deck-drivers' Of course not, this was 100% interest about everything tram .

About the same time as this, or perhaps a bit later, another boy of similar age was just as fascinated with Leeds trams as I was, but probably his school was in the opposite direction to mine and we did not meet until 1944. This boy, whose name was Keith Terry, had the edge on me even then! He knew where to find the dates on the cars that said when the car had last been painted. Keith knew a lot more about Leeds cars then and he still does! His interest in Leeds cars has, like mine, never waned over the last 60 years and when I asked him in 1992, if he could tell me when 272 and 173 were last painted

Plate 36: The top deck 'saloon' of Balcony car 309. In spite of camera shake, this photograph shows the hardly adequate wooden seats that were accepted as normal for two persons up to and during the Second World War. Author.

light blue and '1948-blue' respectively for authenticity in modelling, Keith produced the dates within minutes, and that was over the phone. Such is the attraction of Leeds trams.

Back now to the first few journeys to and from school in 1940. Let me assume that for once we were lucky enough to be warm and dry at the front end upstairs on a Pivotal The last loop down Beckett Street was between Green Road and Nippet Lane at the top of the slope up from Green Road. There was then a short single length before the double track from Nippet Lane came into the single track down Burmantofts Street. In October 1942, Burmantofts Street track was doubled. I remember this being done and watching progress on the large mid-road excavation. Another ex-City of Leeds School boy got on the No.9 here.

One of our constant fears during our journeys to and from Cockburn High School was that we would get on the wrong tram. This was unlikely on the journey from Harehills to Dewsbury Road as we boarded the car almost at its point of departure. However, coming the other way when school finished at 4.00pm, we would dash out of school (glad to be away from there) along Burton Avenue into Dewsbury Road and if there was a car (any car) coming down Dewsbury Road towards the library at Moor Road, we would run this stop-length and hope the robots at Moor Road would delay our intended car just that bit longer so that we could get across to the tram-stop on the Town side of Moor Road. This tram-stop was used by the Middleton cars too, but they were of no concern to us as we had run all the way to the stop, after release from school, concentrating on jumping on the car to Harehills Road(11). Phew! Settle down to compare homework requirements at least until the car got to Leeds Bridge. Homework was forgotten by myself then until we reached York Road, at least, because there would be so much tram interest in the centre of town. Settling down again after York Road on our No.11 to Harehills Road, the car would travel up Burmantofts Street and turn right into Nippet Lane. PANIC!! We had got on the wrong tram in our rush to get away from school and here we were going to a foreign district, Compton Road. The conductor then wondered what the scrat-round was upstairs as we grabbed our satchels and raincoats and slithered downstairs fast before the car could go any further along Nippet Lane. You can imagine the conductor's thoughts.

At the bottom of Burmantofts Street the York Road tracks came in from the left. What track, depots, etc., were up York Road? Wasn't Easy Road up there too? Then the single line down Marsh Lane went off to the left under the railway bridge. Our car went down here on occasions and arrived at Kirkgate just the same as if we had gone down New York Street.

Now, this little area poses a question which my memory will just not answer. I have in my mind a thought that I had 'seen' a single track turning right from facing points in Kirkgate and leading into Harper Street from the direction of Marsh Lane and then turning right again via trailing points into New York Street towards the Central Bus Station, thus providing a duplicate loop to the Yorkshire Penny Bank curve, used by the cars to and from 22-Temple Newsam. We never used the 9-Dewsbury Road route to go to town, so what I think I saw at a much later date was an ordnance sheet of about 1933 which would have showed the track layout in this area as it was before the Harper Street single track became an elongated 'S-bend' when the single track in New York Street was doubled in April 1939. However on most future journeys to school the cars went down New York Street and negotiated Harper Street. The curve from Harper Street into Kirkgate was very sharp and I thought that the Pivotals would have to take it very gently to avoid derailment.

As the car came to the stop at the top of Kirkgate I realised that I was looking in the opposite direction from where Mother and I had stood in New Market Street. This view up Kirkgate towards New Market Street was new to me. The track layout was intriguing. The track my car was on turned left quite sharply and joined with a curve coming from where the Crossgates, Halton and Gipton Estate,(18, 20 and 21 routes respectively), loaded at barriers. A curve from these barriers went left down New York Street. Connecting these two opposite curves from the 18 and 20 barriers was the single track that we were about to join, coming from Call Lane on our left.

As we waited in Kirkgate to load up, a car came out of Call Lane with 10-Compton Road up and I realised here was a length of single track where cars ran both ways. Now I cannot remember for certain but there must have been some control, similar to that on the loops in Beckett Street, so that there was no chance of a head-on collision. It was getting quite light now and our car moved off and turned into Call Lane where the single track branched into double just before the 14-Stanningley curve came round from its loading barrier.. This area was constricted and had 'tight' trackwork in narrow streets and not until I had ridden over the tracks many times, both ways, could I observe 'normal' running of the cars and the 'abnormal', For instance, I never saw a car go from the 20/18 barrier and come round into Call Lane. Was this curve used for routes long closed? Perhaps like Morley or even Wakefield?

Now we were really at Corn Exchange and were seeing the tracks coming in from New Market Street and Vicar Lane, the centre-of-town stops for the Beeston and Elland Road cars, from Harehills and Meanwood respectively. So then round to Duncan Street, and Rawcliffe's. But this time, for the first time, we turned left down Lower Briggate and under the railway bridge past where I had seen that first Middleton car in December, 1938. I had still not had any further clues as to the whereabouts of 255 and certainly not about any other depots. I wondered again if, now we were going into South Leeds, whether I might be lucky and observe any Middletons or any buildings that might look like 'tram sheds'.

Until we reached Duncan Street I had noticed that there were no facing points that required changing electrically by the driver, but I saw that he always had a point iron hooked over or near the hand-brake pillar for use if the bad weather had made the operation of facing points difficult. A typical location was outside Burton's in Duncan Street to turn down Lower Briggate, although I think I remember pointsmen being on hand from Briggate Barriers to keep Boar Lane/Briggate points free of slush, etc.

However, we went under the railway bridge and hardly had the

Plate 37: Car 236 on route 10-Compton Road, having just turned into Nippet Lane from Burmantofts Street. The track to the left went up Beckett Street to Harehills Road. H.B. Priestley/National Tramway Museum Collection.

thoughts about depots gone through my mind when the car came to a triangular junction - the street name to the right was Swinegate. Looking to the right, Ah! look, tram-tracks going into a large building and also going past both sides of the building. Would that be a tramshed? The conductor on our car told me that that building was Swinegate Tram Depot, the largest in Leeds. My my! Mark that down. Must go and look in there, very soon!

Immediately after my seeing that depot the car went over Leeds Bridge. My father had said that the only bridge over the River Aire that the Dewsbury Road cars went over would be Leeds Bridge. Nothing brilliant about the bridge but the 'view' upstream was. There was an array of old sheds on the right bank of the river with some rather dirty-looking single-deck cars with no windows, Even more exciting, some 'cars' with two ends and no bodies, just what appeared to be tipping containers in two halves. What was that place? Somewhere clearly very near to Swinegate Depot so I must get down there to have a long look around. All this was seen in the short time it took to traverse Leeds Bridge and hardly had I absorbed that view than we came to another junction where a pair of tracks went straight ahead.

My car turned right across the path of these tracks and very shortly came to another big junction of tracks at a crossroads. Standing at the robots to our right was a light blue car. Now this was not like any car that I had been close to before. A rather 'smooth' front had two headlights and its number was 264. It must be a Middleton car and the first one that I had seen close to.

Now I knew what 255 would look like. Seven years wondering what 255's shape and colour would be like answered in a few seconds. The robots were red for us and this light blue car came out of that street and turned right on to the tracks in front of us and in the direction we would obviously be going. What a different and up-to-date car 264 was in comparison to the other cars in Leeds except 272 to 274. It had two double seats either side at the front upstairs and the destination 'Middleton' and the route number 12 were below the upper saloon windows, rather like the Converts, i.e. 367 that I had seen at Boar Lane/Briggate about a year previously.

How long the car was and it had bogies, not four wheels. Another thing to mark down! Why on earth didn't these cars come up to our part of Leeds? (They would, in 1942). If all the Middleton cars are like 264 then they are beauties and Stuart Pickford and I must have a ride on them one day. These cars had been in service in Leeds for about 5 to 6 years and it had taken that length of time to see one properly. I must try and see where 264 goes, seeing it's in front of us. The conductor told me that the Leeds end of the Middleton and Hunslet routes was near Swinegate Depot. Ah! I thought, no wonder I hadn't seen any of these cars, except a fleeting glimpse, when I stood at Boar Lane/ Briggate junction!

Minutes later, after the first seeing of 264, this Middleton car turned left and out of my sight at another double-track junction. Which way were we going? Never mind that. Another 'older' sort of car was coming towards us from the route straight ahead. This route actually curved slightly to the left in my view so that only a few hundred yards were visible. The car coming over the junction looked older and although it had 3-Harehills up, I didn't immediately tipple that it was like the cars that we had always let go at Harehills Corner because they were going to 5-Beeston. There was so much to see all at once! The number rang a bell - 371 - and then I realised that the route straight ahead must go to Beeston. I also wondered if it went anywhere else. This car - 371 - had stairs that went up next to the lower saloon, similar to the balcony cars. Something else to mark down and investigate later.

Then we turned left, the same way as the Middleton had gone. In fact I could just see the car almost out of sight up this road we had just turned into. Where's the street name? Ah! Over there on the wall of the public toilets. So this is Dewsbury Road! Hardly had we turned into this road (which was all granite setts for a surface) when I saw another Middleton car appearing to glide down towards us. No bouncing on these cars, no sir! This car had 12-Swinegate up and I have no recollection of its number but I remember thinking it wasn't 255.

Seeing 264 going up Dewsbury Road and then this other Middleton coming down made me realise that we were travelling on the street part of the Middleton route. I wondered how far up this road we would go before having to get off for school. My car followed 264 up this road past a large factory on the left, Hathorne, Davey, Sulzer, and past ends of terrace houses that looked very old.

Concentrating on my first across-town tram journey to a new school - in wartime too - and worrying about what the new school would be like, the last thing that would have been in my thoughts was the Coronation of King George VI on May 12, 1937, about 2 years earlier. Nevertheless, on that date the patriotic residents of two streets near to this tram route in Dewsbury Road vied with each other for the best street decorations and tea to celebrate the Coronation. Purton Street had a tingalairy man making Galway Place green with envy. Remembering the pre-war bright lights, the change to severe wartime conditions was hard to accept as my car went past these street ends. Very shortly after passing here we came to another double junction with a pair of tracks turning left at robots. No sign now of 264. This road on the left was plated as Moor Road and I had to bring myself back to reality and realise I had to get off my car here and walk from here to Burton Avenue and to Cockburn High School. But as my car crossed over Moor Road, another Middleton car was coming towards the robots on Moor Road and its number was 271.

Thanking the conductor for his help, I got off the car along with the rest of the 'across-town' pupils. We had to get off the car here because this stop was the fare-stage for our penny fare from Harehills. The next stop, at Burton Avenue, though next to the school, would have cost three halfpence and we did not have that money. Now, as I was walking along, two things dawned on me. One was that we must have passed over at least five sets of facing-points and had been so busy watching everything around the car that I had not remembered to watch the driver operate the points. Never mind, there will be plenty more runs to Dewsbury Road. My time at Cockburn would be at least three years.

The second thing was that that last Middleton car I saw was 271, the next number to 272, obviously! Now, a great discovery. 254 was a P.35. 255 was the first Middleton and now here was 271 and it must be the last Middleton car! I 'knew' 272, 273, and 274, so what sort of cars were 275, 276, 277, 278 and 279 or even up to 300?

There were, we understood, three London cars in Leeds, and, as previously stated, I did not see the first one until later on in the year. To try and guess what their numbers might be was difficult but it seemed likely that they might follow on in the 27x series. All these Horsfield, Middleton and 272 to 274 numbers had replaced 'old cars' with those numbers (the 'magic two's'). How far up the 27x or into the 28x 'tens' did the London cars go? All very enthralling suppositions! However, these thoughts had to be banished, temporarily, as I had to concentrate on a new school again, new masters and mistresses and girls in the same class. The City of Leeds School had been an all-boys school. Mr George Taylor was the Headmaster of Cockburn who eventually became Director of Education for Leeds.

When eventually I did see my first London car, the first two figures were 27-, implying that the old cars, those with the 'magic two', might start at 280, unless, of course, there were any other cars new to Leeds that I knew nothing about yet with numbers possibly starting at 280 onwards. There were three London cars, and between 275 and 279 inclusive were FIVE numbers! Thus two numbers were either spare or had been given to cars that I knew nothing about. Must keep a good look out for those cars 275 to 279, and I'd better check, on seeing the next London car, exactly what its number is. If the 'old cars' do start at 280, what are they? Are they balcony cars and where are they? These questions were the first about what became a mystery to me! A mystery that I did not solve until 1942. (Chapter 6).

At the junction described on page 62 (bottom) but later in 1940, towards the end of the school year and when I was travelling to school as usual, my car had crossed Leeds Bridge when, much to my surprise I saw a tram of a very strange shape coming into town along these tracks. This strange car, in '272-blue', had small numbers, like 272 and a 25 in a route number box, like 400. Again, asking the help of our conductor produced the surprising answer that the route was from Hunslet and that car was from London. Wow! The whisper was true and here was 27 something - couldn't see the last number properly - and I had seen the car myself.

And so these journeys went on for another three years during which time all manner of tramway discoveries were made, but, fairly soon after those first few journeys across Leeds I decided that I wanted to work at Leeds Tramways amongst the trams when I left school, though in what subject or in what capacity I had no idea.

Eventually, I did see all the London cars and found that their numbers were 277, which was in service on Lawnswood and Roundhay routes, 278 and 279 which I saw on the 25-Hunslet route on my way to school. 275 and 276 remained a mystery until I was able to visit Swinegate Depot, where all sorts of surprises awaited me.

In our first winter, 1940, travelling from Harehills to Dewsbury Road and back, there were four of us travelling each morning, all ex-City of Leeds School pupils. We came home at 4 o'clock, sometimes by different routes. Both journeys had to be by tram as no Leeds bus routes went up Dewsbury Road. I wouldn't have gone by bus anyway, the trams were far too interesting!

As I have said, very often the cars on the early-morning duties were the 318, non-waterproof' or 'empty-top-ends' cars, or henceforth, 'balcony cars'. When we had been travelling for a few weeks and had got used to it, we four 'perishers' (in both senses of the word) would get on the car at Harehills Place, pay our fares downstairs to the conductor and go upstairs, straight through the back and front saloon doors and sit outside at the always empty front end. (See Plate 36) You can imagine the thoughts of the other passengers already inside the top-deck saloon when both doors were opened. I understand that the winter of 1939/1940 was a very hard one. The challenge we gave each other in those winter journeys was to see who could last out longest in the cold at the front of the car. I

CELEBRATING WITH A TINGALAIRY

RIVALRY OF TWO LEEDS STREETS

Colours Flying Despite the Rain.

selves. *And has Purton Street got tingalairy?"*

Purton Street's Denial

In Purton Street it was stoutly denie that any decorations left over from th Jubilee was being used.

"It was all burned," said one of th inhabitants. "Mind you, we didn't expec the Coronation, or we would have kept it."

Two prominent members of the Purto: Street Festivities Committee are Mrs. E Green and Mrs. E. Uttley.

The decorations have been twice ruine by rain since Sunday, and were going u for the third time this morning.

"You should have seen it on Sunday," sai Mrs. Green. "It was lovely. Everybod remarked about it. People came from al round to see, didn't they, Mrs. Uttley?"

"Yes," said Mrs. Utley, "there were crowds They all said Galway Place was nothing tc it. And we have got the school shed for the tea. There was a race for it, and we beat Galway Place.

"Well, you know," said our reporter, "Galway Place haven't got all their decorations out yet. They have a good deal of stuff in reserve."

"So have we," said Mrs. Green, triumphantly. "Lots of it. We haven't put everything out yet, not by a long chalk. And then there's our tingalairy. *Have Galway Place got a tingalairy?* Tell me that?

Our reporter didn't dare.

Plate 38: An article in the Yorkshire Evening Post of 12 May 1937 in connection with celebrations for the Coronation of King George VI. Yorkshire Evening Post.

remember no illness as a result of this activity, but the other passengers were not pleased at our returning to the comparative warmth of the top-deck saloon - SINGLY! This new game didn't last long because the conductor soon realised what was going on and put a stop to it, but I wish I had kept a note of all the cars we travelled on. I suppose one reason for not doing so was the always-underlying thought during our journeys across Leeds, 'I have to go to school and will my homework be in order'?

In 1941 Leeds had two 'important' air raids, one on March 9th when a bomb damaged Swinegate Depot. Another raid was on March 14th when the museum in Park Row was demolished by a direct hit. Leeds was very lucky in comparison to Coventry or Liverpool.

My father was an air raid warden and I would often go with him to the Warden's Post in Ashton Road. When the sirens went we would listen for aircraft engines and watch the searchlights looking for planes. Our aircraft engine noise was always a continuous note and so when we heard WRMM - WRMM - WRMM - WRMM, we knew it was one of theirs - a 'wombling disynchronous engine-note', according to a writer of the time and we wondered where they were going. Tramcar noises were a pleasure to hear and were lasting (we hoped). These aircraft noises were worrying and we hoped that they would not last. They didn't! We never for one moment thought that Leeds would be without its trams. If there had been any inkling that such heresy had been thought of in 1940 (albeit postponed until the war was over), then films would have been brought out from 'under the counter' and everything would have been noted, photographed, listed and 'written down' by the likes of Keith Terry, Jim Soper and myself, whether the Tramways liked it or not. Certain individuals in Leeds City Transport at Swinegate Head Office did not like knowledgeable persons from outside asking questions about the operation of Leeds cars and their system.

In 1941 I didn't suppose for one moment any of us on the Dewsbury Road cars ever thought that the air raid sirens would go during the day. I don't remember any such occurrence. So I carried on swotting up at school and swotting up on Leeds cars and routes. Each of these subjects ran parallel in my life until I felt it was necessary to write down all I had discovered about Leeds cars.

Now, why did I feel I wanted to write down all that I had found out about Leeds Trams? What would I do with all the information so collected? Would it really help me, in any way, if and when I got a job 'amongst the trams'? Or, more likely, was it just straightforward interest to the 'n'th degree?

Certainly the last thing I thought of in 1941/42 was that what I wrote down then would be of historical value half a century later. One cannot imagine these things.

In those days there were no existing lists of cars in Leeds. To be correct, I did not know of any lists that were available to the public. Why should the public want to know, anyway? The Head Office of Leeds City Transport in Swinegate and Kirkstall Works would be bound to know their cars, surely. Therefore I would make up my own list.

It would be an exciting and long-term exercise finding all the cars - I didn't know for certain HOW MANY cars there were! There were bound to be many cars that I hadn't seen or noted, or that I couldn't find or were missing altogether, like 321, 166 or any 280's, respectively. Some would be in Kirkstall Works, or K.D., and I hadn't found that yet.

This then was the incentive; not that an incentive was really necessary to see and get to know the cars. Writing their details down would impress them on my mind.

I knew that the numbers went up to 400, even to 426, but how many more were there? In due course in the next year (1942) Mr Pegram at Swinegate Depot would tell me that car 445 was the highest number. The Book was, therefore, going to be a large one to accommodate all this information without cramming and to allow for unknown factors.

And so it was all written into a large, foolscap-size one and a half inch thick, hard-backed, lined-pages, ledger-type book from Dinsdale's of New Station Street. But this eventually proved to he not wide enough across for all the details and I returned to Dinsdale's in August 1942 in the school holidays, with father's money, to buy another maroon-backed book, size 15 inches x 12 inches approximately, which had enough columns in it to allow full descriptions of Leeds cars and the Hull cars too. It is titled 'Leeds Trams 1 to 477'

I am glad to say that this book is still with me for historical reference, but the first book seems to have vanished without trace. The latest book, of 1942, includes almost everything that was in the first one, but the loss is annoying. Fortunately Andrew Young was able to use both books as some small help for his booklet, 'Leeds Trams - 1932 to 1959'.

As soon as a numbered list is started, i.e. 1 to 445, of whatever subject, then all the items listed therein have to be seen to be written about fully. That would, no doubt, he understood by everybody once they had done it, but I was just starting and I had to learn. Right! How to find out where No.1 was, what it was and everything about it.

'Never mind about No.1' said my mother, 'deal with the cars you have seen and know, then deal with the cars that you see, as you see them and write the details of those down'. Mother knew all about writing things down as she was well-versed in Inland Revenue procedures. So I had a good instructor once I got home after looking for cars, depots, yards, etc. and after doing all my homework.

By now, by virtue of seeing lots of cars on journeys to and from school, I was getting to know the types of cars and their equipment, what routes they went on, even the first and last numbers of the various types of car although not in every case by any means. I hadn't found all the depots yet and I didn't know anyone who could tell me more about the cars or even about Leeds City Transport.

So, all I had learned, so far, had been by my own observations and personal effort, outside on the routes, not by visiting Tramways property and asking questions. What I really needed was to get behind the scenes of the operation of the trams. To do this I felt I had to 'knock on depot or office doors' if I could find them and if those persons behind those doors would answer the knocking of a 15 year old youngster!

Plate 39: Car No. 1 - The first Pivotal car to be built by Brush at Loughborough in 1926. Courtesy Brush, Loughborough..

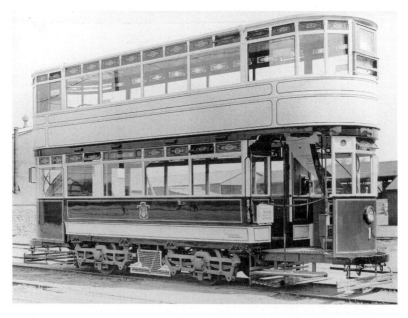

Chapter Four

SECRETS, DISCOVERIES AND 'LEARNING THE TRAMS'

There are ways and means of finding people who can answer questions. About now, late 1941, my father thought it might help in many ways (and be cheaper for him in the long run) if I was allowed to have a bike, then, in present-day parlance I could be a 'Heineken' and get to places I could not normally afford to go. I had learnt to ride a bicycle in 1937 but it was not considered safe for me to have one of my own until I was at secondary school. Perhaps being evacuated to Lincoln had something to do with permission being granted for me to own a bike. I think it was called parental apprehensive confidence!

So on 14 December 1941, father and I walked down to Roundhay Road and then down to Roseville Road, where, on the left-hand side just past Bayswater Road was a cycle-shop. My father must have been in this shop earlier and found a machine that he thought would be right for me, because, once inside, there was this immaculate Hercules 3-speed Roadster, with a gearcase, and it was to cost father three pounds, ten shillings (£3.50). I could polish the badge on the front stem too.

Now, as the proud owner of a bike I could explore. (See Plate 16) There was no thought then of getting leg-cramp after a cycle ride. I could visit all those places I had seen from the tram to school or that I had been told about. I could even ride along a tram route and find out where it went and what depots, if any, or any other exciting 'things tram' were along the line.

One idea in my mind then was to find the secret places of Leeds

Plate 40: The Head Office of Leeds City Transport, Swinegate about 1952. West Yorkshire Archives Service, Wakefield.

Tramways. There must be secret places and wherever or whatever they were, they would only be secret to me! Leeds Tramways would, of course, know all about their own property, but I wasn't asking them in this case, I wanted to find these places myself, where passenger cars did not run, like the place I saw from Leeds Bridge on that early journey to Cockburn High School.

Two or three places that were far from secret but to me they might just as well have been were remote (from Harehills) termini. For instance 19-Lower Wortley, 16-New Inn and Whingate, 20-Halton, 18-Crossgates, 21-Gipton Estate or 22-Temple Newsam, anywhere on 14-Stanningley, 6(ex 24)-Elland Road toward Churwell, and 5-Beeston Hill to Beeston. Any others could wait - this lot was going to take some time to find and explore. There were, of course, many more secret places that I didn't even know about. 1942 was going to be a year of discovery, I thought.

The idea of going into the Head Office of Leeds City Transport to ask for information (even if I'd known where it was) had never occurred to me! In those days to a young lad, even the words 'Head Office' meant some majestic place young lads were not allowed in or if they went in they were chased out, sharpish.

My mother again came to the rescue about these places by giving me a suggestion about the depots that did the trick very nicely. She said,

> 'When you go to these depots, etc., there must be a Depot Manager or similar. Why don't you march straight in, ask to see him and tell him of your interest and ask him if you may look around'.

Mother then added,

> 'there's no need to be afraid of these people, if you act straightforwardly and openly. Usually people will help if they see that there is a genuine interest. In any case, they are <u>all the same in the bath</u>, you know!'

Well, armed with that sort of advice, I decided my first visit to any premises of Leeds City Transport should be to the 'largest depot in Leeds', the one I had seen from the tram on the journey to Cockburn High School, i.e. Swinegate Depot. It must have been on a Saturday morning about March, 1942 when I walked in the high door of the depot. My! What a place. A long single track along the left-hand-side of the building and umpteen tracks curving off to the right at right-angles to the single 'through' track. There didn't seem to be a bit of rail on this through track that wasn't made of points or a crossing. This was an immediate impression. When I turned the corner, on the

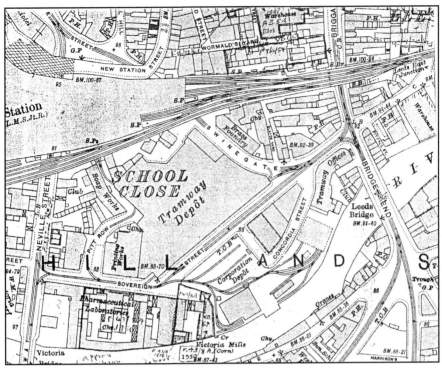

Map 4: Swinegate Depot and Area in 1933. By kind permission of the Ordnance Survey, Southampton.

right of what looked like the 'offices' there were lines of cars between gantries with people cleaning the top decks from these gantries.

However, my objective was the Depot Manager and having asked where this gentleman's office was, I knocked on the door marked Depot Foreman and was answered by a loud 'come in'. Thus I met Jim Wade (Mr Wade to me), He was gruff, offhand but very kind. He asked quite a lot of questions about my interest in Leeds cars, about my school, my parents and what I wanted to do when I left school. My reply that I wanted to work amongst the trams, produced the surprising (to me) reply, 'Oh! you want to work across the road, then?'

On my questioning the phrase 'across the road', he explained, 'Across there is Tramways Head Office'. So I rapidly found out where the Head Office was and putting two and two together also very quickly, I deduced that all the property, 'across the road' from the Head Office along the River Aire side must be Leeds Tramway's property because of the single-deck 'cars' I had seen from the car on that journey to school. That means there is a very big area around here to explore, with permission.

Then Mr Wade took me out of his office into the depot at the Swinegate end of the building. We stood about the middle of a square formed by the offices, the end of the gantries by the side of the tracks, the small walls near the parked Bedford van and the outside wall of the depot.

Plate 41: Swinegate Depot about 1938. This treasure of a photograph, albeit posed, brings back the excitement and delight I felt every time I visited this depot. See Plate 116. Geoffrey Hilditch.

In December, 1938 I thought that standing at Boar Lane/Briggate was marvellous, but standing in this position in Swinegate Depot was absolute bliss! Lots and lots of cars in long lines on the 15 tracks of the Swinegate half of the depot and there appeared to be just as many tracks on the far side of the Bedford van. The photograph of the cars at the head of tracks 8 to 15 vividly reminds me of my thoughts this day. (Plate 41)

About track eight, there was a yardman's cabin squeezed between the through track and the depot wall and some cycle racks nearby too. Mr Wade took me to this cabin and introduced me to Mr Pegram. He was an older man and when he was told by Mr Wade what I was up to, he picked up a board with squares and numbers on it and took me into the middle of the depot, into the 'neutral zone' of plain concrete floor that formed the division of the depot into two halves. The track that came into the depot from Swinegate had fifteen tracks turning to the right from it. The track that came into the depot from the Sovereign Street end had another fifteen tracks turning to the left from it. And there were cars on all these tracks, but the tracks were not full. I had, of course, thanked Mr Wade who asked me to see him before I left the Depot.

Mr Pegram explained the board which was a diagrammatic plan of the depot, The squares on it represented each car 'space' on each track and in the appropriate spaces on that Saturday morning were the numbers of the cars actually in residence as it were. The car numbers were written in pencil so that they could be easily changed when shunting was carried out at any time of the day. We went down the slight slope to the bottom of the depot towards track 30. A very short track with track 29, similarly short. Track 29 reminded me of the then current song 'Chattanooga Choo Choo'. Mr Pegram was just telling me all about the depot and what there was behind it when I found 297, which literally stopped me in my tracks on that track 23. 'Wow!' One of the cars of yesteryear with a number beginning with the 'magic two'!

Mr Pegram explained that 297 was the breakdown car, it had track brakes (slipper was the word used, I think). The car had been used on 24-Churwell and 15-Rodley, both closed now, and the car could go anywhere on the system. Not now in passenger service, of course, 297 had all the gear inside to re-rail a car and chains to tow cars out of service.

Fancy finding one of the old cars on my first visit to any depot, any information or sightings or discovery of any of these magic cars was an exciting event. It was as though I had come into actual contact with a bit of Leeds Tramways of an era well before I had any knowledge of the cars. Pre-1926 at least. How I wished 297 could 'talk' to me Why, I wondered, was 297 chosen as the breakdown car? It could have been any one of the old cars. Perhaps I should be thankful that the choice fell on a 'magic two'.

While we were looking at 297, Mr Pegram opened a large, sliding door through which a track went, by the side of track 23. I thought, 'now what secrets are out there?' with great anticipation. Once through this door the track ran along what I judged to be a very old, narrow street at the back of some equally-old buildings and then vanished underneath the railway arches. These were the secret places I had hoped to find. (See Plate 42)

What a place this was! Empty except for gas-tar engines, lots of scurrying noises inside and railway engines in steam at Leeds Station on the viaduct above. One would never expect tram-tracks to go into a place like this.

We came back into the main depot where Mr Pegram said,

'If you would like to look around the depot, do so, but be very careful if you look on the cars. They are very high up on some of the tracks where the walkways are well below the track level'.

No Health and Safety problems in those days, just common sense. And so I was let loose in Swinegate Depot! What an experience for a tram-mad lad. I was thrilled to bits. The depot was able to take about 180 cars. I'd never seen so many cars all together- even though the depot wasn't full. I felt a very privileged person!

This would be early 1942 and the smells of the cars, electrical, mechanical and wood smells, I have never forgotten. I was very careful as I walked up each track between the cars so that in future visits - and there were plenty - 'they' would give me a 'clearance certificate' as it were. This visit was the time I began to call the cars 'my trams' because I looked on the cars as personal things. They gave me great delight all the time. The fact that nobody, except my parents, knew this did not worry me at all, neither did the knowledge that the Tramways had never heard of a 15 year old boy who thought that the trams were 'his'. It wouldn't have made any difference to Tramways anyway. They had a job to do and they got on with it regardless of enthusiastic youngsters.

Still in the depot, the space between tracks was about four feet lower than rail level and so I was able to look under the cars to see the motors, brakes, lifeguard rods and levers, wheels and axles and get dirty hands too because all these things were touchable. Not to worry, it wasn't dirty dirt, it was tram dirt and that was allowable. Then to climb up on to some of the cars and stand still inside or upstairs and imagine who the cars had carried. Some cars would have run on those routes now closed including South Accomm. How I wished the cars could answer my umpteen questions. One question that I asked Mr Pegram was: 'What was the highest number on Leeds cars?' '445' was the answer, 'an L.C.T. Piv.'

I didn't find any more balcony cars whose number began with the 'magic two', though there were quite a few 300's down the tracks, particularly on tracks 16 onwards.

There were one or two Middleton cars, but no sign of 255, Pivotals of all types, Beeston cars, Converts and Horsfields too. I found this particularly exciting. On any of the cars in this depot I could stand at the controller and imagine that I was driving the car. It was possible that day to pretend I was driving a Balcony car 306. Then get off 306 and get up on Beeston car 383. What a difference in 'feel' between 383's controller and brakes to a fairly simple layout on 306. Off 383 and on to Horsfield 252. Here was a tremendous difference from 306 and 383. To round off this 'trying' of cars, I climbed up on to a Middleton car, 260. Never mind the number, examine the car. Sit on the front seats upstairs for the first time and see-out-front all round. Then back downstairs and sit in the driving position. Look in the outside mirror and experience the length of the car.

During this exciting exploration of the cars and the depot, it dawned on me that if I was to walk down to the bottom of the tracks in the depths of the depot and if the wall was straight, perhaps I could

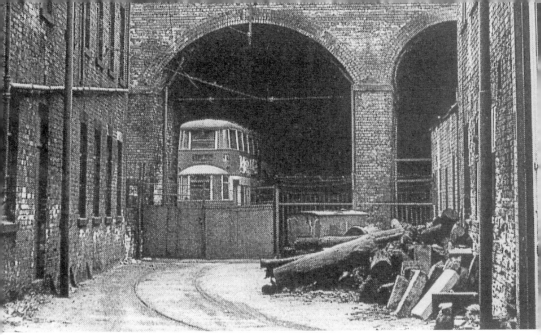

Plate 42: The Arches at the back of Swinegate Depot. One of the secret places of Leeds Tramways. The ex-London Feltham car was photographed here in 29 July 1955, but in 1942, under the Arches under Leeds City Station was considered most secret. Keith Terry.

see the end of most of the 30 tracks of cars. If each of the 30 tracks had a car at the end, that would be a line-up of cars in a secret place that nobody else other than Swinegate staff would be able to look at. That would be exciting. Again, it would only be a secret to me, of course, but I was always on the look-out for secret tramcar places.

So dirty hands wiped over again with rags found in the aisles between the cars, I walked to the back of the depot. The shape of the back of the depot did not allow me to see along 30 tracks, but it was a magic, silent world, just myself and lines of cars side by side between the steelwork of gantries and depot structures. Just imagine how I could have made this day even more exciting if I had been able, with a magic wand, to extract stories from any of the cars. Never mind, thanks to a very down-to-earth Depot Foreman the very fact of my being here with full permission, on my own and only 15 years old, was unbelievable. I wished I could have shared my excitement with my parents, but wait until I tell them about everything when I get home. Oh, boy! This was a most memorable adventure! I hoped it would be the first of many. On later visits I met Depot Foreman Albert Howells who was another gruff person and on the opposite shift to Mr Wade, but even he was kind enough when I was introduced to him.

On leaving the depot, for safety reasons, Mr Pegram was glad to know that I was leaving and possibly for other reasons too. I sought Mr Wade out in his office and thanked him for an exciting visit. He said I could come anytime but always to see Mr Pegram first before going to look at cars. Common sense and safety.

This first visit to Swinegate Depot was a first class adventure. I had found 297 and lots of other cars but not 255. When I had got to know Mr Wade and Mr Pegram better during the course of 1942, one outcome was that Stuart Pickford and myself were able to photograph 297.

Later on in 1942, on Sunday 25 October at 11.45am, Mr Wade agreed to drive 297 out from Swinegate Depot into Sovereign Street and place the car near the entrance to the Permanent Way Yard so that the car could be photographed by Stuart Pickford. This photograph, a copyright of Stuart's, shows Jim Wade, myself and another depot man on the 'empty-top-end' of 297 with 14-Pudsey up. Birkett, the man standing on the road was always known as Birkett, not mister or by a Christian name.

Thinking back fifty-seven years, I suppose it must have been quite something for Jim Wade and his lads to take time off to run a car out of the depot for Stuart and myself to photograph it. Stuart was nearly 18 years and I was nearly 16 years old. We must have felt a very privileged pair of young lads. Jim Wade did it again for me to photograph P.35-204 (see Plate 45) when it was newly-painted in wartime khaki in Sovereign Street on or just after February 27 1943.

My mother's advice was being proven!

Also on the first visit to Swinegate Depot I learnt the way the cars were referred to by L.C.T. staff. For instance car 255 would always be stated two, five five. Not two fifty five or two hundred and fifty five. Cars 200 or 400 were always two hundred or four hundred. Car 111 was always one one one. Car 49 was forty nine, not four nine. Car 301 was three-oh-one, not three hundred and one. Later, the Hull car 446 was referred to as four four six and the first Feltham car in Leeds was always two oh nine nine. This convention has lasted throughout the years and has no doubt, influenced my way of referring to any object which was referred to by number.

During the actual exercise of photographing 297, it occurred to me that I might take the bull by the horns and ask Mr Wade if it would be possible to photograph 255 in the same position as 297. He did not jump on me for asking such a perhaps impertinent question, but suggested that if, on a Sunday, we came down to Swinegate Depot and asked Mr Pegram the whereabouts of 255, on 25-Hunslet, of course, we would be able to wait for it to come back to Swinegate,

Plate 43: Car 297. The first 'magic two' that I discovered a few minutes before discovering the Arches in Plate 42. 297 was photographed in Sovereign Street on 25 October 1942. Stuart Pickford.

ride on it to Thwaite Gate and photograph it there.

This was an ideal solution. It saved Mr Wade taking a Middleton car through all the points of the depot fans and out into Sovereign Street over track which was not normally used for other than shunting or football specials. A derailment or any other damage sustained by 255 as a result of an unofficial photocall would have brought the wrath of the General Manager down on Mr Wade. So his suggestion was welcomed from all aspects. It would give us an unexpected opportunity to see and ride on 255 for the first time and to explore a strange route and see Hunslet Depot. An exciting prospect indeed. The next Sunday after taking 297's photograph that we were both free was on 15 November 1942. So, down to Swinegate Depot again where Mr Pegram told us when to expect 255 back in Swinegate itself.

Patience! Until 255 put its nose round the corner of Swinegate from Bridge End and came to the stop outside the Depot. Here was the car at last. Even seeing the number 255 on the cream panel under the driver's window was exciting. It had been nine years since father had told me about

Plate 44: Car 388 at Meanwood terminus about 1949. This was the type of car that left Easterly Road at 0755 hrs every workday morning to get me to work on time. R.F. Mack.

Plate 45: Car 204 was driven into Sovereign Street by Jim Wade, in a similar way to 297 in Plate 43, on or about 27 February 1943. 204 is in full wartime livery, khaki paint overall with white fenders, headlamp masks and anti-blast netting. Author.

255 and now we could not only see the car, we were going to ride on it.

Bearing in mind what we wanted to do at the terminus, we thought it not only polite but wise to introduce ourselves to the driver and ask his assistance. Would we be able to photograph 255 with him and his conductress at Thwaite Gate? They were both happy to oblige and so Stuart and I went upstairs to see-out-front to enjoy the car and a strange route. It was wartime, no traffic so there was no problem about standing in the middle of a road junction at Thwaite Gate and taking our time to photograph the car. I have no recollection about how or where I got the film. Possibly Pearson and Denham's in Bond Street. I used Mother's camera.

This was our first ride on a Middleton car and even though it was on Hunslet, what a ride. No bouncing over points or junctions like Great Wilson Street and Meadow Lane. Just a smooth absorption of steel shock. I couldn't compare any other car in Leeds to 255.

We knew the driver was comfortable in his cabin, so, never mind the motors or controllers, trucks or brakes, we just thoroughly enjoyed the car. Even the wheel-noise over joints sounded like a railway carriage-di dum, di dum. Yes, Sir! This was a proper tramcar.

Excitement caused a degree of camera-shake but we got our photographs and then enjoyed the journey back to Swinegate. On the right-hand side of Hunslet Road, there was South Accommodation Road. The route closed in 1936 and it is still causing me some research problems, because I have never yet seen any photographs of cars on this tight single-track-and-loop line.

Eventually, I found all the Middletons in Swinegate on subsequent visits and Stuart Pickford and I travelled up and down to Middleton soon afterwards, sat upstairs at the front both ways. Thanks mainly to Mr Wade, we had had another exciting adventure on the trams.

In 1991 we visited Blackpool en route from our Coast-to-Coast walk exertions in the Lake District. This visit was an opportunity to photograph and ride on Blackpool's cars which had to include a ride at the front upstairs on 724 to Bispham. We were immediately back, in memory, to that first ride on 255, 49 years earlier. Such is the memory or presence of Leeds cars.

In 1942 the dispersal of cars every night from Swinegate Depot to outlying areas to avoid possible bomb damage was undertaken by depot and yard staff. Most cars were taken to the long track in Low Fields Road by the side of Elland Road Football Ground. Some were taken to Middleton.

Gradually, since I had had my bike, my parents had become accustomed to my having 'rides out' in the daylight and in the blackout, with tram investigations as the purpose. Even my bike lamp had a mask with a slit in it, but, not having a windscreen to look

Plate 46: Car 255 with driver and conductress at Thwaite Gate, Hunslet, on 15 November, 1942. Standing in the roadway to take the photograph was no hazard. There were few vehicles and even less petrol in wartime. Author.

through, I found riding in the blackout most exciting. My parents were not surprised when I asked permission to ride down to Swinegate Depot to watch the 'dispersal cars' go out.

Arriving at Swinegate, I put my bike in the racks near Mr Pegram's cabin, saw Mr Pegram or his counterpart and stood and took in the movements of a considerable number of cars. One of the staff had come down to Swinegate when Stanley Road Depot closed and eventually as I got to know other yard staff I was able to ride with them to Low Fields Road, on the platform with the driver. And in the blackout too. For me this was almost the peak of excitement and ambition! At long last to be able to ride with the driver - and remembering the numbers of times I had sat at the front of cars from Harehills to Town wishing that I could do just that. There is a time and place!

The ultimate in excitement was when, on Elland Road itself, I was unofficially allowed to drive the cars and even into Low Fields Road siding itself and take the car right up to the stationary cars down the line.

There were, of course, no lights on on the roads and the lights in the cars were put out so that people would not try to get on the cars. The blackout helped to disguise the 'driver' too. All the drivers on this duty knew about my travelling with them, but they never let-on and pulled my leg no-end when we were travelling back to Swinegate in the L.C.T. Bedford van, FNW 7xx, I think it was.

I have never forgotten how to drive trams and it is still just as exciting when an authorised opportunity occurs at Crich, as on November 3rd 1991. (See Introduction).

Earlier in 1942, towards April, whilst still at school, I thought that because I had learnt a lot about the cars, any happenings on Leeds Tramways would be known about, if not by word then by observations. How wrong can one be!

I was walking up Lower Briggate from Swinegate and was passing Dyson's. I looked over towards Duncan Street and couldn't understand what I was seeing! There in Duncan Street next to Burton's and coming this way was a tram of a strange shape and painted in the wartime khaki green. Where on earth had that come from?

There was a '9' in the route number box at the front of the top deck and 'Dewsbury Road' in the separate destination box above the driver's windscreen. There was a Leeds Coat of Arms on the side. Strangest of all, in small numerals, like 272, was the car number under the driver's windscreen - 446! Now, only recently in Swinegate

Plate 47: Cars 270 and 163 parked at Middleton after being brought up from Swinegate Depot to this dispersal point in case of damage by air raids. Middleton cars like 270 never had anti-blast netting fixed. The drivers were well known to me but not their names. Author.

Depot, Mr Pegram had told me that Pivotal car 445 was the highest car number in Leeds, so what was this most un-Leeds-looking car doing here with 446 on its dash, made of wood panels of all things? By virtue of the Coat of Arms it looked as though the car had come to stay!

So I stopped still whilst this car came round into Lower Briggate and stopped at Watson Cairns. It set off down towards Leeds Bridge with a most non-Leeds noise. I do not remember if it had netting on the windows. Most likely it would have had. Straight away I ran back down to Swinegate Depot and fortunately found Mr Pegram in his box and asked him if he knew anything about this 'funny car 446'. 'Oh, yes', he said, 'It's from Hull and there's quite a few more in Kirkstall Works'. Of course, I didn't know where Kirkstall Works was, much less was I able to go there in the recent past.

No doubt, if it had been possible, I should have known about the Hull cars. But I'd only just found Swinegate Depot... ! As it was, I thought, 'Nobody tells me anything these days'. An unfair thought, I suppose, for who would think about saying anything to a 15 year old? I didn't think much of this 446 on first sight and I didn't change my opinions in the future. The car looked like those pre-war toys that supposedly were made to look like, say, London buses, but were

Plate 48: Bernard, left, who taught me to drive trams on dispersal duties from Swinegate Depot in 1942. See Plate 29. W.A. Camwell/National Tramway Museum Collection.

made of tin and 'made in Japan'... Nevertheless that information from Mr Pegram caused me to prepare a few more pages in the Book, because, being forewarned, more space for description would be required for these cars as, it was said, no two Hull cars were absolutely alike. I was remembering the phrase - 'from Hull, Hell and Halifax, good Lord deliver us'.

Eventually, after we had got used to the Hull cars, when I heard one setting off from Harehills Sorting Office, I knew the noise was a Hull car, but is was not possible to identify which one as I looked down Milan Road to watch it pass my line of sight.

Reflecting later on the Hull cars running in Leeds and the sighting of 446, I wondered who the person was who made the decision to number the Hull cars 446 onwards, as well as such numbers that would be required if any other cars were either built by or brought into Leeds.

Also, was the same person, or the same office, responsible earlier for the 'As' on the 'A-cars' and for giving 255 its identity, similarly for 272 to 279? Was this numbering decided from records held by the Works Superintendent at Kirkstall Works?

If the procedure for allocating fleet numbers to the tramcars may be presumed to have been undertaken at Kirkstall Works, once the number was placed on the dashes and/or the sides, inside the cars on the bulkheads and upstairs on the destination indicator woodwork, each was then forever identified by Kirkstall Works as, say, 180 throughout its life with Leeds Tramways.

All electric tramcars in Leeds right from the beginning have had Fleet numbers only to identify each car. When motor cars came on to the roads about 1903 they were all required to display a Registration Letter and Number, issued by the Motor Taxation Office which, in Leeds, was at 5, South Parade. The motor vehicle registration letters allocated to Leeds in the early days were: U, NW, UA, UB, UG and UM. The Lord Mayor's official car had the registration number HUB 1 which was issued from the Licence Department, South Parade by my father. The official car eventually acquired the registration number U 1.

In 1911 when the first trolleybuses were put into service on Whitehall Road, like the trams, they only had fleet numbers, 501 onwards. From 1921 onwards, trolleybuses not only had fleet numbers, they also had registration letters and numbers, e.g. 510 was NW2734, even though the Act of Parliament of 28 November 1910 stated that:-

> 'Trolley vehicles shall not be deemed to be light locomotives within the meaning of the Locomotives on Highways Act 1896... nor shall they be deemed to be motor cars within the meaning of the Motor Car Act 1903 and neither the regulations made under that Act nor the enactments mentioned in the schedule to the Locomotives on Highways Act 1896, nor the Locomotives Act 1898 shall apply to trolley vehicles.'

Is this *Leeds Corporation Act* 1910, 10 Edw.7 and 1 Geo.5,

Plate 49: *Ex-Hull Car 449, in full wartime livery at Thwaite Gate, outside Hunslet Depot on 12 April 1942.* M.J. O'Connor

Ch.CXLIV, the reason why tramcars in Leeds were never required to have registration numbers of the form allocated to buses and other road vehicles?

I never did discover anything about this hidden, but important creation of identity for Leeds cars.

At that time, 1942, I wondered why it was necessary to have cars from Hull, of all places, in Leeds. I knew that three cars had arrived from London, but they looked like proper tramcars, not something made out of Meccano and covered in wood panels.

Very shortly after that surprise, another awaited me. By now, I thought I knew the first and last numbers of cars of different types, except perhaps those in the 280 to 369 range. There was still a great deal of investigation to do in this number range.

The cars in this range were amongst the oldest tramcars still in Leeds, some were the remaining cars whose number began with the 'magic two'. These cars could have been scrapped or, I hoped, hidden away in some secret place that I had yet to discover, or they could even be being considered for further conversions. However, I thought that by now I knew the cars that had been converted from balcony cars to fully-enclosed cars like 348 that I saw at Boar Lane/Briggate junction in December 1938.

For example, cars converted were 332, 340, 341 and 343 to 369, any cars in the range 280 to 369 not converted were still straightforward balcony cars, wherever they may be shedded and if they were still alive.

So, strangely enough, again I was walking up Lower Briggate and again I had got to Dyson's being very wary now in case I came across 447 or its companions. But it wasn't 44-anything I saw this time, it was a Convert, newly-painted in khaki. A Convert painted khaki was a strange sight anyway but this car was 339!

The last I thought I knew, or assumed I knew of this car was that it was a balcony car in blue. So, never mind any other vehicles on the road, dash across Lower Briggate and have a closer look. It stopped at the robots at Burton's. As I got near I could smell and see the new paint. Very smart khaki paint, white paint in all the wartime places and polished (varnished) wood seats downstairs. This duty must have been its first trip out. 339 was without track brakes and therefore precluded from Beeston, etc. It was on 9-Dewsbury Road.

Standing in Duncan Street and reflecting on 339, a newly-painted, perhaps re-built car, even in wartime, combined with the work necessary to try and transform cars from Hull into presentable Leeds cars, I thought I must try and find out where all this work was being carried out. Wherever it was, there must be a lot going on there. Its capability would be fascinating to see and learn about. Who knows what I might find in a place like that. Perhaps this was a cheeky thought on my part for it was Leeds City Transport's business and all part and parcel of Tramway's activities and policy, nothing to do with me. 'Yes, it had something to do with me', I told myself. The tramcars were as much my cars as theirs and, if I took my mother's advice again, there was no limit, wartime or not, to what I might find out. So back I went to Swinegate Depot, (no time like the present), to seek out Mr Wade or Mr Howells. Mr Wade happened to be on duty which was perhaps as well, because I had got to know him a bit better and he knew I meant business.

I asked him where cars were built or repaired or serviced, etc. He knew very well that if he told me about 'the Works' he would be inflicting a very curious but very, very interested youngster on to Mr Daggett at Kirkstall Road Works. But

Plate 50: A copy of the Act of Parliament *for Leeds Corporation, 1910. 10 Edw. 7 and 1 Geo5. relating to the registration of tramcars as not being motor cars.* Leeds Local and Family History Library.

that is exactly what he did by phoning Mr Daggett and arranging for me to go down there on a Saturday morning. I was ever so pleased and could hardly wait to ride home and tell my parents. Where was the Works on Kirkstall Road? In my excitement I never thought to ask Mr Wade.

To find out I had to wait till next day until I could question Inspector Crossley at Briggate Barriers on my way home from school. He told me,

'Get on a No. 4 car, Haddon Place or Hawksworth Road, at Harehills and stay on it until the end of Wellington Street where the car will turn right into another road leading to West Street / Kirkstall Road junction. Get off the car at this junction, just past the factory of Fairbairn Lawson Coombe Barbour. Walk along Kirkstall Road on the left-hand side and you will see a crossover and soon after that there

is a single track turning left, from the Kirkstall Road tracks, into the Works. The entrance is a narrow one, but there is a Yardman who will take you into the Works'.

I thought 'It's rather like a story from 'Grimm's Fairy Tales'. It sounded just as magic!

The very next Saturday morning, down at Harehills Corner, I waited for a No.4 to come round from Clock Buildings, got on and went straight upstairs and sat at the front on the left-hand-side of the destination box. i.e. on the curved seat over the stair well. The journey to town was familiar, of course, and even along Boar Lane to City Square was becoming so, but riding on a car along Wellington Street past the Central Station was entirely new.

As Mr Crossley said, the car turned right towards West Street and it was time to get off. I think the tram fare was two pence (school). My excitement grew as I walked along Kirkstall Road past factory walls on my left and the double tram-track in the roadway, I came to the cross-over and a car-length past this were the points for the turn-in to the Works. It was a fairly narrow entrance and the yardman's office was on the right. I explained my appointment to him and to confirm it he rang somebody. 'Please come with me' . My excitement mounting, we stepped through a small door built into the big door at the Works entrance. Wow! A huge building with umpteen tracks coming off one in-going track. And the cars... Oh boy!, steady on, wait for Mr Daggett. The Yardman took me across track after track to the offices in the middle of the building, knocked on a door and I was shown into an office to meet a gentleman in a brown trilby hat and a smart suit - Mr Daggett, the Works Superintendent.

Mr Daggett was kind enough to put me at ease straight away. He knew I was excited to be amongst the trams and asked many questions about my interest in the cars and some searching questions about my intent on leaving school. When I told him that I firmly intended working amongst the trams he almost repeated Jim Wade's words,

> *'Ah! probably on the engineering side at Head Office. Have you been in there yet to look round the Drawing Office?'*

On my negative reply, Mr Daggett suggested that that was what I ought to do next. But how?, I thought. Here was another world beginning to open up. I had no idea what a Drawing Office did, but judging by Mr Daggett's immediate reference to it, he seemed to be saying that that was the place in Tramways for me to aim for on

Plate 51: The new tram track reservation at City Square on 21 March 1938. Cars 64 and 204 are seen. H.B. Priestley/National Tramway Museum Collection.

leaving school. This, I realised, was only seventeen months away.

Bringing me back to reality after I had been a year ahead of myself as it were, Mr Daggett said,

> *'Now, I'm sure you would like to look round the Works, wouldn't you? Come on then'.*

Can you imagine how I felt? Once more a very privileged young lad. There was so much to see. Cars up on lifts, cars being painted, cars being repaired, new motors, new or refurbished trucks, a Pivotal with its trucks in front of it. Controllers being worked upon and with their innards exposed. A P.22 truck was next to its body. It was so strange to me to see cars with their equipment being worked upon next to the car. Almost like when I was in Seacroft Hospital for scarlet fever.

We came to the traverser where a car was being driven on to it. The whole thing moved on two rails in its well taking the car sideways across the Works to another section for further work to be done on it. Some cars in the body shop were almost skeletons and some were parked, obviously having just come out of the paint-shop. One of these was a Hull Car, 449, I think. (See Plate 49) There were others there, still in their tatty Hull colours.

Mr Daggett took me across the traverser to have a look under a car that was up on the lifts. Different 'secrets' now, of the cars themselves! It was explained to me that this car was having a thorough examination of the steel frame under the body and the truck was undergoing a similar thorough overhaul at the same time.

The wheels were being re-tyred too.

Some cars had obviously been in accidents, the damage was 'as smashed' and I wondered where would one start to repair a stoved-in front-end? I cannot remember details of all cars that I saw, I was far too interested in everything. I felt that here were cars that I knew on the road and here they were being worked upon. It was almost as though the cars' spirits were being laid bare. However, this visit took me right in deep amongst the trams and I relished every minute of it. Mr Daggett explained everything and although some things were beyond my 'ken', I learnt a great deal and the whole morning was unforgettable. A very, very exciting time. I also wondered how anyone got to the position of Superintendent in a Works such as this. How did Mr Daggett start in Tramways? When eventually, we returned to Mr Daggett's office, I thanked him for a very exciting visit and also for taking the time to take me right round the works. He told me to 'come again, anytime', but to advise his office on arrival so that checks could be made that everything was safe for me to be on site. I was certainly going to come again, as often as possible without being a nuisance. In hindsight, I'd have liked to have worked there on a Saturday morning, but in those days such an idea was unheard of. As it was, when I left the works, where I could happily have stayed all day, I walked down to the stop at the end of Kirkstall Road and recall thinking - almost out loud - when I saw the cars that were in service: 'Ah knaw summat abaht thee! I know where you all

go for servicing, overhaul and repairs'.

I felt that I had been privy to a big secret of Leeds Tramways and, apart from Mother and Father, I should keep my own counsel until I was actually working at Tramways (and, perhaps, after that too) in whatever capacity.

It had been a most interesting, exciting and satisfying Saturday morning.

Plate 52: Car No. 11 and opponent, Car No. 431. Where would one start to repair this kind of damage?
Yorkshire Post.

Chapter Five

A Depot is a Magnet

About this time, on 27 April 1942, probably as a result of this visit to Kirkstall Works, my mother wrote, on my behalf, to the General Manager of Leeds City Transport, Mr W.Vane Morland, and asked how I should go about applying for a job amongst the trams, because 'a tram depot is a magnet that never fails to attract him'

This 'depot-door' attraction is well illustrated in two photographs. One is by H.B. Priestley of 26 May 1939 and another by W.A. Camwell on 26 May 1938. Mr Priestley's view is along the single track in Stanley Road approaching the first points of the track fan. The doors are open on the left-hand side of the picture. I never needed an invitation to look through any depot door, even before I ever had permission to enter any depots. Once past the doors the cars on the tracks inside were viewed with intense delight and if one or two cars were being moved so much the better.

The second 'depot-door' photograph is the classic one that all tram-mad youngsters dreamed about. (See Plate 29) Mr Camwell was able to arrange that the last car in on each track was driven out just outside the doors with the result that here is a photograph of seven cars that I can look at time and time again and never get tired of it.

With this view it isn't necessary to look through the doors, the cars are there, outside, 'looking for you' as it were.

Stanley Road Depot was the only depot, that I knew, where the depot track-fan was in the roadway and outside the depot. All the other depots in Leeds were entered through a tall doorway and the track-fans were inside the building.

If a tramcar could be watched either going into or coming out of

Plate 53: The letterheading of Leeds City Transport, from a letter of 29 April 1942 from Mr W Vane Morland to my mother. Author.

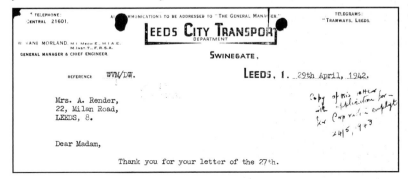

Plate 54: Stanley Road Depot track fan, the only one in Leeds that was in the roadway. This view, taken on 26 May 1939, shows the points to the four tracks of the Roundhay Electric Tramway depot of 1894 and the three points of the 1910 extension. H.B. Priestley/National Tramway Museum Collection.

the doors of any depot it was always an exciting thing. The doors seemed only just wide enough and tall enough to let the car through. No passengers were allowed to remain on a car that was depot-bound, so here was another situation like that of never normally being allowed to ride on the driver's platform. I always wanted to ride on a car into a depot for the very reason that a depot was not part of the public tramway. Once inside the depot doors the car was in a secret place.

To return to my mother's letter to Mr W. Vane Morland. The General Manager replied personally and I still have the letter in which he referred me to the Juvenile Employment Bureau. I didn't hear from them until 24 May 1943, when they sent me a form.

In those twelve months - the wait had to be endured as 15 years was much too young for Corporation Service - I tried to get to know as much as possible about Leeds trams for my Book and in so doing get to know a lot about Leeds.

My parents now allowed me to ride my bike to school when it was fine. The tram fare so saved was ten pence per week and thus I was able to discover where Hunslet, Balm Road, Dewsbury Road, Beeston, Elland Road, Lower Wortley, Whingate and New Inn termini were. I had some very long rides home after school and even longer ones at weekends.

Now that I could ride to school, my parents thought it would be better for me if I was able to have a proper dinner at midday as the school dinners in wartime were not considered adequate for a growing lad! So it was arranged that I would cycle to 'the Bayswaters' off Roundhay Road for dinner. Plenty of time in school dinner-time to do this and a time when cars could be seen if I chose my cycle route appropriately.

Part of that route was down Dewsbury Road to Holmes Street and Kidacre Street and across a railway track at the bottom of Holmes Street. I remember often stopping to watch a small steam locomotive cross over Holmes Street. The track was part of a gasworks railway and the locomotive's name was 'Blenkinsop.'

I had recently found Kirkstall Works. Whilst in the Works (it became known to us later as 'K.D.' for Kirkstall Depot.) Mr Daggett had said there were depots at Hunslet, Bramley and Torre Road and disused ones at Guiseley, Morley and at the top of Vicar Lane. I couldn't imagine where that building was, so I'd have to explore there carefully! Both Guiseley and Morley had been in use in my early years but they were too far away for us in those days.

During these longer rides of exploration, I found that the track in Stoney Rock Lane had been doubled. In some parts of this roadway now the rails were so close to the kerb-edge that not even a cyclist could pass between the kerb and a tramcar. The track layout at the Kirkgate - Call Lane constricted junction was also improved about this time - October, 1942. The single-track in Call Lane between the

Plate 55: Guiseley Depot in 1915 and 83 years later on 31 March 1998, the name 'Leeds City Tramways' in the side wall remains. Leeds City Tramways/Author.

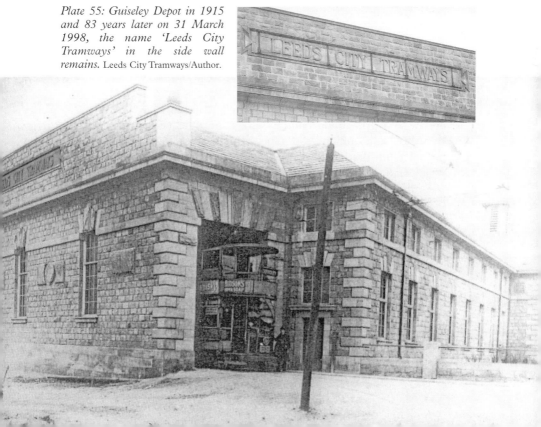

'14' curve and Kirkgate was doubled. Although this improved tramway running, the cars completely blocked this short roadway. Such delay as there was with the single track was immediately removed when the doubling was complete. It made my journey to school that bit easier.

I remember standing and watching the re-laying activity in Call Lane. I knew nothing about trackwork renewal then, but I did wonder where and by whom the layout was designed, not realising that such designs were done in the Drawing Office in Head Office, 'across the road' from Swinegate Depot. I would be working in that Drawing Office in about 17 months time, but I had no idea of that in April, 1942.

Further afield, I rode as far as Bramley and found Bramley Depot where a new roundabout had caused a re-design of the trackwork leading into the depot which was of the 'tall-narrow-windows-with-semi-circular-windows-at-the-top' style. Probably because of the distance from home this depot gave me the feeling of being secret. On looking through the tall narrow doorway, set at an angle to Henconner Lane, it was clear to me that only Horsfields were stabled here and this was a novelty. Two cars, which were individuals, were 'living and working' from this depot, 165 with a Maley and Taunton truck (see Plate 78) and 166 with Crompton West controllers. I didn't find either of these cars on this visit but on the second visit not long afterwards 166 was 'at home'.

Whilst mentioning controllers, I am reminded of the feel of the different controllers and their handles. On my visits to Swinegate Depot I was able to stand at the controllers of various cars - to imagine that I was driving the cars. In reality all I did was to hold the controller handle on each car. The Metropolitan Vickers handles were solid, wooden knobbed and low-slung near the controller top and with a grip-filling handle, whilst the Dick, Kerr handles were thinner, higher-off-the-top type, which required the hand to be placed palm-first on the series notches and then pull the handle, which had a black, bakelite knob, round into parallel. All this was assuming that the reversing-handle was in position, the circuit-breaker was off at both ends and nobody heard me practising.
Normally the reversing handles and the air-brake handles (on Horsfields) were always taken off the cars for safety's sake once the cars had been left down the tracks.

I have often wondered since, where these handles (about 180?) were stored until the cars were scheduled for duty again. In a big box, perhaps, or on numbered racks? I don't remember seeing a car's number stamped on either type of handle. Another hidden little mystery that may never be solved?

The controllers on the Horsfields were much more up-market than those on the Pivotals. The majority had chromed tops and chrome handles with a black knob, be they B.T-H. or G.E.C. A Horsfield could hardly have had an 'old-fashioned' controller like the Dick, Kerrs, could it? The next stage of exploration in this area was to ride along the long drag from Bramley to the 14-Stanningley terminus at Half Mile Lane, which was, I discovered, also the terminus of the 44 bus route to Stanningley from Osmondthorpe, which went past the top of 'my' road, Milan Road. Further on from Half Mile Lane, the tracks went to Cohen's Foundry. Rusty tracks here, so I assumed that few cars ever went to Cohen's. This was very close to Richardshaw Lane and, keep it quiet, the Boundary of Bradford. What a name was given to this little area - Stanningley Bottoms. However, the 14-Pudsey route turned sharp left here up under the railway bridge, which was as far on the Pudsey route as I ever have been. Pudsey, of course, is where 't'birds fly backards to keep t'muck out of their eyes' and where Len Hutton, the cricketer, lived. Bradford was foreign country and totally out of the question. Didn't they only have balcony cars there?

Now, having got this far along a strange route and being very pleased with myself at discovering this long '14', which way to go back home? Well, I thought to myself, I might as well follow the 44 bus, which was all very well, going generally downhill to Kirkstall. Here crosseth the 4-Hawksworth Road tram route. Slowly up from Kirkstall and I came to North Lane and the terminus of the 27-Cardigan Road route with the single track for Cricket Ground 'Special Cars' coming along North Lane into Headingley Lane and the 1-Lawnswood route. From here I followed the roads that I had ridden over, sitting on Father's knee, years ago on trips to the tennis

Plate 56: Car 253 is seen in Bramley Depot entrance at an angle to Henconner Lane on 16 January 1949. R.B. Parr.

Plate 57: Car 351, converted from a balcony car, is at 27-Cardigan Road terminus in 1938. Note the cream band below the top deck windows. H.B. Priestley/National Tramway Museum Collection.

courts at Lawnswood. The 44 bus route was an educative route from a tram point of view. It crossed no less than eight roads that had or had had tram routes on them and passed three separate termini of the cars. The eight roads were York Road, Roundhay Road, Chapeltown Road, Meanwood Road, Headingley Lane, North Lane, Commercial Road, Kirkstall and Broad Lane, Bramley. Route numbers: 17, 18, 20, 21, 22, 3, 2, 6, 1, 27, 4 and ex-15 respectively. The termini passed were 10-Compton Road, 27-Cardigan Road and 14-Half Mile Lane. This was, therefore, a very interesting route to travel on, or would have been, had we been able to afford it then. Thank goodness for my bike.

On further visits throughout 1942 and 1943 to Kirkstall Works

Plate 58: Cars 237 and 171 on the tramway reservation towards Bramley Town End. Car 171 has a double fender due to larger diameter wheels being fitted on trial about 1942. R.F. Mack.

Plate 59: The remains of the lower deck of Pivotal car 104 at Kirkstall Works about 5 July 1942. Stuart Pickford's diary (Plate 60) confirms the event. Keith Terry.

(K.D.) I was aware that a new car was being built and was to be given the number 104 to replace a Pivotal that was burned out at the Soldiers' Field between Oakwood and Roundhay on July 3rd, 1942. The new 104, being built something like 272, was a wartime, severe, austerity version of that car and predominantly based at Bramley Depot. Pivotal Car 104 never went near Stanningley - Pivs. were not allowed on that route (14) in my time.

Stuart Pickford and myself photographed the new 104, the 'Austerity Car' as it was called, at Half Mile Lane shortly after it entered service in December, 1943. I never did find out why 104 remained on the '14' route. The new 104 had, I was surprised to note, a vertical-panelled wooden dash. Surely K.D. had not been influenced by the Hull cars headed by 446.

TRAMCAR ON FIRE

Swift Work Saves Passengers on a Leeds Track

Owing to the speed with which a tramcar was cleared of its passengers when it caught fire on the express track between Oakwood and Roundhay, Leeds, nobody was injured.

Driver Weatherhead, of Chapeltown, found that the power had failed and that smoke was issuing from the rear of the vehicle. By the time the passengers had alighted the tram was well ablaze, and in the end only a skeleton was left, the upper structure being completely gutted. There were about 90 passengers on board at the time.

Firemen were in attendance for an hour, but they were handicapped by the distance of the tram from a water main.

Corporation officials describe the fire as one of the worst of its kind experienced, and as a rare accident. The tram was a 1928 model.

Plate 60: Stuart Pickford's diary page for 3 July 1942 records the fire on care 104. Stuart Pickford.

However, my overall knowledge of Leeds and the cars was improving gradually, thanks to Father's idea of my having a bike. No doubt this accumulating knowledge, though scanty at this time, would help when the time came for interviews for a job amongst the trams, or so I thought!! My bike was proving most valuable. Lots more 'places-tram' were being discovered as well as many entirely unknown details and districts of Leeds.

Plate 61: The site of the fire which engulfed Pivotal car 104 on the tramway reservation in Princes Avenue, Roundhay on 3 July 1942. Stuart Pickford.

Plate 62: The replacement car 104, loosely named the Austerity Car, photographed with Stuart Pickford at Half Mile Lane, Stanningley on 29 January 1943. Author.

Plate 63: Car 254, the last of the hundred Horsfields build by Brush of Loughborough in 1931/32 at the Clock Cinema, Easterly Road, Harehills in 1943. This poor photograph emphasises the empty and dismal conditions that were an accepted way of life in the depths of the Second World War in my part of Leeds. Author.

Chapter Six

THE MOST REWARDING DISCOVERY

s I said in Chapter 4, I thought, with great expectancy, that 1942 was going to be a year of tramway discovery. Up to about April, the year most certainly had been and the rest of the year looked like being even more exciting.

For some time now since my first visit to Swinegate Depot I had assumed the existence of other balcony cars, similar to 297, whose numbers began with the 'magic two', without knowing for certain if such cars were alive or what numbers they would have.

Surely these cars could only have the numbers from 280 to 299 at most because I knew that the last London HR2 was 279. I had been trying to find where cars 280 to 299 were simply because there were still blank spaces in my Book, between 279 and 300 (apart from 297, of course). I did not know at that time that there was any historical significance in these missing cars. Without pennies for the tram fares and without a bike it had not been possible to run around Leeds in a haphazard fashion looking for ghost trams. My parents would not have let me do anything of the sort, especially in wartime.

Plate 64: The official party at the formal opening of Torre Road Depot and Garage on 8 April 1937. Standing left to right: The Lord Mayor of Leeds, Alderman Tom Coombs and Sir Josiah Stamp. Sitting left to right: W. Vane Morland, General manager, Mr Hayes, a lady (name unknown), Alderman F. Leach, Chairman, Transport Committee. Leeds City Transport/West Yorkshire Archives Service, Wakefield.

Plate 65: Torre Road Tram Depot and Bus Garage, almost complete in March 1937. Leeds City Transport/West Yorkshire Archives Service, Wakefield.

The condition of the only car I had found from the missing range, 297, gave me a clue as to what sort any of these mystery cars might look like. In any case, because they would have numbers beginning with a two, this made them like 297 excitingly old and indeed, unique in Leeds.

I had no idea where on the system such old balcony cars might be. However, the rumour that they were still 'alive' from the beginning of the war made me very curious.

The description 'old cars' here was my overall term for the cars that had been scrapped or those that should have been scrapped, but were not, before I was old enough to understand and record the cars for the first time in my then present day of 1939 onwards. (Chapter 1)

I cannot remember with any certainty where I first heard that some old Leeds cars might still be out of service and stored somewhere. I did not think to ask any further questions at the time. This kind of self-inflicted lack of thought occurred a few times until it dawned on me to 'think round corners' and get the full story about things, first time.

The niggle about these 'old cars' remained at the back of my increasingly investigative mind until I felt that the time and circumstances were right to make the effort to find this missing part of the continuity of the Leeds cars. As for the other rumour about a 'separate set of numbered cars' (Chapter 1), what on earth could they be - if they existed at all?

Where does one start on such a search? I had never done anything like this before, so I had a problem. However, help was at hand though I didn't know it. On one of my visits to Swinegate Depot I happened to mention to Mr Wade my lack of knowledge about these old cars.

His immediate surprising reply was, 'Well, have you been to Torre Road?' No, I hadn't discovered that depot yet because I did not know where it was. My eternal thanks must be given to Mr Wade for telling me about Torre Road and its location, off York road.

This depot, therefore, was in Leeds 9 and we lived in Leeds 8. By today's standards and impressions of distance Milan Road to Torre Road is just up the road by car, but in 1942 York Road was a strange area and a long way away.

I did not really think that I would find anything out of the ordinary at Torre Road, in spite of Mr Wade's statement. He had also said that the depot had only been in use about five years, so I reasoned that a new depot would have been purpose built for a given number of service cars and, therefore, there would be no room to 'hide' old balcony cars. However, the Depot would be another exciting place to find and examine, so I determined with parental permission, to ride over to Torre Road on the next Saturday. School would have to be endured until then.

Cycling along Harehills Lane on my Hercules bike with the badge on the front head brightly polished, I passed the 10-Compton Road tram terminus and rode up the hill to the Hillcrest Cinema (very appropriately named, I've just realised), then down Lupton Avenue and as I started to freewheel downhill, I thought that the long white building that I could see at the bottom of this road might be the depot and garage. As I got closer there was a tram-size doorway in this building, two in fact, and a track entering each one.

The approach to a strange depot was always with a feeling of anticipation. Certainly that was so this day because to see a track going in (or coming out) of both doors suggested an interesting track layout inside. I had noticed double tracks in Lupton Avenue from York Road going into single line past the Nabisco Factory and turning to my right into Torre Road itself. The continuation of the building down Torre Road was obviously the bus garage because two

Plate 66: Dejected looking Balcony cars at Torre Road Shed in a similar position to how I found them in 1942, with the Depot Foreman, right, and his assistant.
Yorkshire Post.

or three buses were parked at a far entrance.

Having recently had the successful experience of entering Swinegate Depot and meeting Jim Wade, I had resolved to do the same at Torre Road. This tram depot, of course, was far smaller than Swinegate and the track layout was much different. There were two track fans inside the building, which in itself was interesting because no other depot that I had found in Leeds had this. The top tall doorway was the exit, the bottom one was the entry, thus the cars did a loop in and out of the depot. There was even a siding inside too - space was not wasted here.

All this I took in as I rode into the exit doorway and put my bike against the wall next to the stub track which came off the siding. I was taking another leaf out of my mother's instruction book (Chapter 4).

Whilst looking for the Depot Foreman's office to the left of the exit doorway an overalled older man with flat cap came towards me with an expression on his face that said: 'What do you want?' However, on introducing myself and saying that Mr Wade at Swinegate had suggested that I visit Torre Road to investigate old cars, this gentleman took me to the office I was looking for, thus I met Mr Downey, the Depot Foreman. The name of his assistant escapes my memory now. Both gentlemen were later photographed by the Yorkshire Post looking at the balcony cars on Track 7 at the Top Shed. Interest by Mr Downey in my visit was confirmed by his asking me why I was concerned to find the old cars. I suppose, in hindsight, that he knew all about the old cars that were on his patch, he was most likely involved in putting them there in the first place - all part of his job, no doubt! So why on earth should anyone be bothered about finding discarded old trams?

Explaining about my overall interest in Leeds Tramways and that I wanted to work amongst the trams when I left school, I asked Mr Downey if he could tell me where I could find any cars with numbers between 280 and 299. My second question about the rumoured second set of numbered cars, i.e. those with an 'A' after the number produced the surprising reply:

'They're all in the shed up there!' Excitement par excellence! But where was up there?'

My excitement must have showed because the Foreman then said: 'Have a look round, with pleasure, but watch out for car and bus movements'. He then directed me, after I had looked at the service cars, to go through the door at the bottom of this depot, down the steps into the Bus Garage and then to go outside into the bus parking area where I would see the Top Shed, on higher ground, away from

Plate 67: Crich at night. Part of the depot at the National Tramway Museum, Crich, Derbyshire, showing Leeds car 399 and cars from other undertakings on 10 October 1992. In the 1940s we never thought that any Leeds cars would end up in a museum! See Plates 113 and 114. Author/National Tramway Museum.

the bus park. Thanking him and being mindful of incoming cars, I looked at all the cars in the depot. The capacity when full was about 70-80 cars as I remember, mainly Pivotals with an occasional Horsfield (P.35). Certainly no Hull cars yet and, no Middletons. They were totally unheard of at Torre! No P.22s either. Having gone through the cars and found all in order as it were, I went to the entry end of the Depot and just stood there, near the access door to the Bus Garage and looked at all the cars again '...a depot is a magnet' wrote my mother. How right she was and even now when I visit the Tramway Museum at Crich and see the cars from umpteen different systems in the tram sheds there, the magnetism returns. It hasn't really gone away - it's kept in place by a keeper made of photographs, models and memories!

Returning to earth from a tramway heaven, I pushed open the door to the bus garage and was jolted back to the reality of the opposition to the trams as I looked almost over the roofs of the buses in the garage. This was the first time I had ever been in a bus 'shed'. Looking at the buses as I came down the steps from the tram level, I found them to be interesting, yes! and I was aware of the different body styles, mostly by courtesy of C.H. Roe of Crossgates but, being very tram-biased I passed by to the other side of the garage and outside to the bus parking area.

There were a number of buses here and I think I remember seeing 131 (ANW 674) with its 'London 1941' plaque on the panel below the front window of the driver's cab. This plaque was a commemoration of the bus's visit to London on hire to London Transport to help out there because of buses lost in the Blitz.

Whilst looking at these buses, my eyes in the back of my head said: 'Turn around and look up there' So I did as my excited eyes demanded and there on higher ground some distance away was the Top Shed and in front, facing the bus garage were three balcony cars outside the shed. There were three others further over near the front of the shed. All were of the 318 type which, in all probability I would have ridden on in 1940 on journeys to Cockburn High School. Even from a distance three of the cars near the end of the shed had white bands round their dashes implying that they had been in service at the beginning of the war and the blackout.

More excitement now! Are the really old cars going to be in this shed? Does the track to this shed come off the York Road tracks? If I'd looked that bit further down Lupton Avenue towards York Road as I cycled into Torre Road itself I would have seen the points that led into the Top Shed yard - but I didn't - I was far too busy looking at the entrance (or car exit) to the depot. I did not know that there were any points in such a position anyway, because the very existence of the Top Shed was unknown to me.

However, making sure that no buses were moving about, I ran from the bus parking area up to this Top Shed, hardly able to hold my curiosity. The three cars at the end of the track nearest the bus garage were 301 at the very end, then 312 and 308. Leeds trams were

Plate 68: Cars 301, 312 and 308 on Track 7 at Torre Road Top Shed in 1942 before the rest of the cars in Plate 66 were driven on (see Plate 18). Author.

never allowed to get into such a poor condition as these three cars, so how long had they been parked up here and outdoors? I had the three cars already in my Book so I must have seen them in service in 1940 onwards. Why were they dumped up here? Were they past repairable redemption? because they were not what I called the 'old cars', their numbers were past 300. Too many questions for a person with little tramway knowledge to answer!

Looking past the three cars, there was another track next to 301's track which had seven works cars or vehicles on it. Thoughts flashing through my excited mind as I stood near 301 were that the main issue at this shed was about cars, although out of service, that would have numbers in sequence with the rest of the fleet, i.e. cars whose

Plate 69: Torre Road Top Shed on 14 July 1997 with approximate postions of the tracks of 1942 superimposed. Author.

numbers and descriptions might close the gap in my Book between 279 and 300. It was exciting to think that I had never seen what amounted to a secret group of cars. I did not, at this stage consider the second set of numbered cars i.e. the 'A-cars', although the Depot Foreman had said that they were all up here. By 'A-cars' did he mean this second set as well? Certainly the second set had not created a gap anywhere in my Book. How could they have done? They were outside the normal sequence of Leeds car numbering. More questions, no answers...yet. Perhaps I thought of this second set as Will O' the Wisps that would appear as a further surprise.

I wondered if that surprise would be this day?

If so, would I find these shadowy 'A-cars' in this Top Shed?

What would their numbers be?

How many would there be and where would the 'A' be?

At that time I did not know enough history about these Will O' the Wisps to understand why they were called 'A-cars'.

Right! Enough thinking, now to recording. Walking along 301's track towards the front of the Top Shed I could see the access track from Lupton Avenue coming up to the shed with tracks coming off it including this one with the three cars on it. As I turned the corner of the shed, there were three more cars outside the shed - and two of

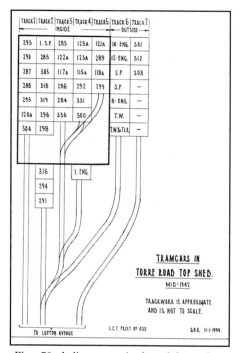

TRAMCARS IN
TORRE ROAD TOP SHED.
MID-1942

TRACKWORK IS APPROXIMATE.
AND IS NOT TO SCALE.

L.C.T. PRINT Nº 433   G.B.L. 11-1-1999.

Plate 70: A diagrammatic plan of the tracks at Torre Road Top Shed with the numbers of the cars drawn as I found them in 1942. See Plate 112. Author.

them were 'magic twos'– 294 and 291 with 316 next to the shed doors. It was so exciting to see these two cars with numbers near to 297. Whatever can be inside?

Before succumbing to this urge to see inside I decided to draw out the tracks first, like Mr Pegram's board at Swinegate Depot, then put the car numbers in their correct positions. Then I could enjoy the strangeness of the cars and let the significance of this occasion sink in.

The points in Lupton Avenue for the access to the Top Shed were trailing towards Torre Road, requiring cars to be reversed into the yard and up to the shed. Towards the shed Track 7 (numbering from left to right facing the front) branched right from the access track about half way between the Lupton Avenue gate and the shed to become a long track. This track had 308, 312 and 301 on it and looked as if it had been added later to the original layout to give a greater car storage capacity.

A horrible thought occurred to me at that moment that I remember very well. Were these cars at the Top Shed placed up here waiting to be scrapped as soon as possible along with many others in due course. Was the political thought that buses were better already simmering in the City Fathers' deep-down plans for after the war. (The war would be won, of course! Nobody had any doubts about that!)

Continuing up the access track towards the Top Shed, this track became Track 1 and went straight into the Shed. The doors were all closed but I noticed a small personnel door on the right-hand side of the front. Track 2 branched right off Track 1 in front of the shed and then went straight in. Track 3 then branched right off Track 2 and also went straight in. From Track 3 outside the shed a short stub branched right, stopping in front of the shed doors but in line with Track 4 inside. Also from Track 3 between the points for the stub track and the points for Track 2, Track 6 branched right and then curved left to run outside the right-hand side of the Shed, close to the shed wall. This track had the Works cars on it.

Now, I had not been inside the shed yet but to keep the continuity of this trackwork description, Track 4 and Track 5 branched right off Track 3 inside, reminding me of the similar track layout in Bramley Depot.

Having got the track layout recorded, now to put the car numbers on the outside Tracks 2, 4,6 and 7 down. Now things began to be even more exciting, There was a Works car outside on Track 4, but I wondered if that small door that I had seen earlier was open. Turn the brass-loop handle that was flush with the face of the doors and push! Yes, it was open. Step over the bottom door-frame and look in awe!

'Magic twos' and five lines of old cars.

'My my! Look at these cars! and feel the old atmosphere and the silence!'

I stood still in my tracks, totally surprised to have found a shed full of cars that until very recently I had had no idea of their existence. On the tracks right in front of me were 299 and 300 and to my left were 335, 298 and 304. These were the front cars of the five tracks inside the Shed. I couldn't see the numbers of the other cars, it was too dark and the cars were tightly placed. What a place to be in. Mr Wade was right. Five lines of historical Leeds cars and I had no previous historical research knowledge.

Never mind, take all these cars in like the proverbial dustbin and decide what to do first! The shed was gloomy, so were the cars standing there tight-fender. I could almost hear them saying: 'We're so glad to see someone who appreciates us. We've just been dumped here and left in silence - after giving 30 years of Service in Leeds.'

The obvious first thing to do was to draw out the tracks in the shed and then, the exciting part, to go to each car and put its number on the plan. Walk now over the points for Track 4 to 299 on Track 5.

299 was the second 'magic two' I had found inside and the fourth found today. How many more are here today?

Come on now, concentrate on 299, walk by its weary side, note the old form of Coat of Arms and the woe-begone once-cream paint under its weatherboard. From half-way along the side of 299, the second car on Track 5 looked different in the vestibule to the well-known shape of the 300s still in service. Different even to 299. As I slowly walked past the rear dash of 299, on this different car the first number I could see was a ONE!

A split-second thought - a balcony car whose number began with a ONE? Surely there aren't any. But here was one. The next number on its dash was also a ONE! The next number was an eight and there

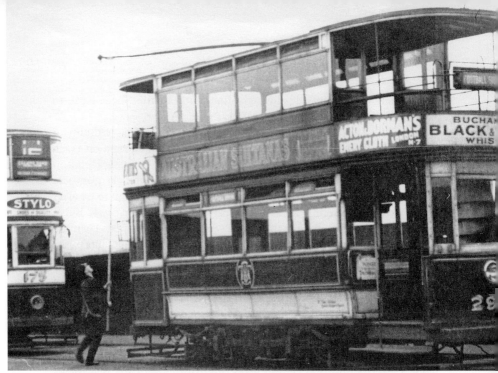

Plate 71: Car 299, seen here at Low Fields as a Football Ground Special on 19 March 1938, but which was one of the discarded cars that I found in Torre Road Top Shed in 1942. H.B. Priestley/National Tramway Museum Collection.

was the 'A' after the eight. Now this really was a discovery! I had found my first 'A-car'. If only I had realised it I was catching up with history.

Continuing towards the back of the shed, shielding my excited eyes from the cars on Track 4, the next car was a 'magic two', 289 and behind this was another 'A-car', 121A. These 'A-cars' were fascinating to see, so completely different from any other cars in Leeds.

Two 'magic twos' and two 'A-cars' on Track 5 already and there were still four tracks of cars to look at. At the back of Track 4 was another 'A-car' 125A with 123A and 115A in front (see Plate 70). Five 'A cars' now, this is unbelievable! How many more? 292, 331 and 300 completed Track 4.

The aisle between Tracks 4 and 3 was the furthest from windows and particularly dark. However, back from the front car 335 there were five treasures, 284, 286, 117A, 122A (see Plate 75) and 283. 283 was the lowest 'magic two' number so far found here, 'there's only three more cars between London HR2 279", I thought.

At the back of Track 3 I paused in the exciting business of recording totally unknown cars and just stood there, listening to the historical silence! Also thinking how lucky I was to be here in the first place. Even at the back of Swinegate Depot the silence was there but that silence was alive. This silence was a stillness caused by rejection;

a silence rarely experienced in later life.

283 was placed tight up against the back wall so I had to return to the front doors to walk between Tracks 1 and 2. On Track 2, 298 was first, then 296, 319, 318, 305, 285 and a Works car. Coming back along Track 1 were no less than five magic twos', 293, 290, 287, 288 and 295 with 'A-car' 120A before 304. (See Plate 121)

What an experience here this day! Sixteen 'magic twos' and eight 'A-cars' all found at once. Also eleven 300s and various works vehicles. A total of thirty-five balcony cars in and around this Top Shed, What a discovery! I felt more than privileged, almost honoured at being allowed to find these secret gems of a part of Leeds Tramways past. This time, my mother's advice had been really proven. Phew! after all the rumours and wondering if or where, here they were! But there were still three cars missing.

All the 'magic twos' from 283 to 299 were now 'alive' and accounted for with none missing, an astonishing fact in itself. Not only were the remaining 'magic twos' here but possibly all the remaining 'A-cars' (eight) were here also. Of course, there may be other 'A-cars' hidden away elsewhere in L.C.T.'s property of which I knew nothing yet. Nevertheless, what a treasure-house I had discovered on this day of surprises.

It did not matter one bit that no one else had the slightest interest in a shed full of old tramcars, least of all any L.C.T. staff. I had actually found the cars whose existence had been only the subject of rumour and conjecture outside the previously impenetrable bounds of Leeds City Tramways administration. This discovery was a success never to be forgotten.

I wish, in hindsight, that I had had the experience of thinking round corners, and had asked the Depot Foreman about when, how, why and by whom the cars had arrived and been placed in and around the Shed. I also could have asked him when the Top Shed was built and the tracks laid in. In 1999 these would be automatic questions, but as a 15 year old...?

A clue about when the 'magic twos'

Plate 72: Car 298 in Duncan Street about 1936. Yorkshire Post.

and 'A-cars' had last run in service may have been the lack of white bands round the dashes. These white bands were put on all service cars with similar dashes at the beginning of the war due to the resulting black-out requirements. If these cars were not used from 1940 onwards, I wondered where they had been hidden away, assuming that the Top Shed was only recently built?

Well now, having recorded the cars I stood back against the doors just to enjoy looking at these old cars. But where were 280, 281 and 282? Were they hidden away somewhere else or had they been scrapped before 1939? I didn't know enough about Leeds tramcar history to able to answer my question. The three cars still left a gap in my Book and it was to be many years before I learned the full story about them.

Whilst concentrating on taking the numbers of the 'A-cars' and 'magic twos', it struck me that the overall appearance of some of the cars gave me a totally different impression from any of the balcony cars that I had seen in service.

Why, I wondered? What was the difference between these cars and the others that gave me this impression? An example was the appearance of 290 on Track 1 and the appearance of 298 on Track 2. Was it because certain cars here were of an earlier origin? I had not had the experience of this possibility before. The cars like 290 seemed to exude an older atmosphere, a Great War atmosphere

Plate 73: Car 281 was one of the three cars, 280-282, missing from Torre Road Top Shed in 1942. I did not know then that all these cars had been scrapped by 1931. David Gladwin.

Plate 74: Car 290 at Kirkstall Works about 1928/1929. The car was built in the Works in 1912 and was another of the old cars I found in Torre Road Top Shed in 1942. Leeds Local and Family History Library.

Plate 75: Car 122A on Track 30 of Swinegate Depot on 19 May 1937. Compare the vestibule with that of 297 in Plate 43. H.B. Priestley/National Tramway Museum Collection.

which I could feel in that shed. This may have been due to my being often told by parents about home conditions during and after that war, only about twenty years previously.

I felt that this atmosphere or impression that the cars were transmitting to me, which seemed to be one of dispirited resignation, was very hard to comprehend. This impression, in all its intensity, has stayed with me through the years, but even now it is still difficult to describe. My father had been a prisoner-of-war in 1918 but only rarely would he talk about conditions there.

This strange feeling - which might be said to be a form of psychic history - caused me to compare such old cars as 290 with one of the later ones, 298 say, and 297. 297 was still alive and had given me present-day impressions.

There was a marked difference between the construction of the driver's vestibules and roundness of the ends between certain cars. Even in the gloom of the Top Shed it was possible to see a difference between 290 and 298 from my stance between 304 and 298. 290 was well down on Track 1 so I had to dodge about a bit to do this comparison. Looking again at 290's front I wondered too how the vestibules on 290 or 298 compared with those on 'A-cars'. The vertical pillars on the windscreen were narrowly spaced on 290 whereas 298 had a wider-framed windscreen, similar to 297.

I looked at the vestibules on 122A towards the back of Track 3 and I could see 290 from 122A across the front of 285 on Track 2. 298 was five cars in front of 285. Another dodge about and I found the front vestibule windows on 122A and 290 are both narrow. More checks on Track 2 on the front of 296 which was the same as 298. Round the front of 298 again to check the fronts of 295 and 293 on Track 1. Both wide windscreens. What about 292 on Track 4 which meant a further dodge to the doors and down to behind 331. Ah! 292's vestibule front is narrow like 290's. Better check 291 outside through the personnel door. 291 was similar to 290 and 292. Now back inside to think!

Does this difference in vestibules mean that 293 was the first car of a modified later design? Similarly were the cars 283 to 292 (or even 280-282 if they were still alive) an older design of cars, always assuming the possibly erroneous thought that the higher the number the newer the car. My knowledge of the old Leeds cars was far too limited to give myself proper answers to these questions. It would also be many years before I learned the full story about these designs too. However, these observations made me think that if narrower windscreens indicated much older cars then cars 283 to 292 and the 'A-cars' could be the only cars left alive of what I called the really old cars. If so, and the rest had been scrapped, were these 24 the only cars that had been reprieved by wartime directives? Thus I had very likely found a link with Leeds Tramways' past only three years before that link would be severed forever. In 1942 such severance could not be imagined, however.

In 1999 this historical link can be proven. The picture in Plate 76 of Car 118 in Briggate in 1917 shows how the car 118A in this Shed looked when it was in service and had the large numbers. I stood on this car in 1942 and found the photograph in 1995. Time-travelling backwards for 53 years in memory and for a further 25 years backwards in history gives me a very strange impression of I was there. Perhaps in 1999 I can now imagine it was indeed possible to be with 118 in that photograph, in the way described in the paragraphs on the next page.

The fascination of Leeds tramcars sometimes shows itself in

Plate 76: Car 118 in Briggate in service in 1917. This car became 118A in 1927 when the English Electric pivotals arrived and, along with 122A in Plate 75, was found in Torre Road Top Shed in 1942. J. Valentine.

extraordinary ways! Psychic history again?

Back to the Top Shed in 1942. I noticed that the stairs went up differently on some of the cars.

122A for instance had stairs going up like the Pivotals 290 and 298's stairs went up the opposite way, like 318 on my school journeys in 1940.

In hindsight now I wish I had been able to photograph these cars, but, in 1942 it wasn't possible.

My exploration of this Top Shed was nearly complete - as far as I was able - so once again I turned to face the cars here and let my imagination take over. The cars here were those that would have travelled to Harehills, maybe I had ridden on them when I was too young to take note of the cars. These cars would have been part of the standard cars in Leeds for my past fifteen years and before then too. Those that had gone had only done so when new cars took their place. The Pivotals came in 1926/27 and other new cars up to 1935.

Today I was back in time and into those old photographs of Leeds, but here was the subject-matter of those photographs. I went upstairs and into some of those dusty and rusty empty-ends. This time they felt empty and discarded. I tried to imagine the folk who would have

Plate 77: Car 118 in Briggate in 1917.
J. Valentine

sat there and the times through which they travelled.

Sometimes when looking at 1917 period photographs showing the trams in Leeds, I put a magnifying glass in a position about three inches above the photograph, then put my eyes close to the glass, then put my hands by the side of my eyes - à la horse blinkers. This way the present world is shut out and if I concentrate very hard it is possible to imagine that I am with the photographer in 1917 or so.

This day at Torre Road I had no need of a magnifying glass, the old cars and the 'A-cars' were real and I was there, with them. It was so exciting to have found what I thought was probably the last secret place on Leeds Tramways. It was only secret to me, of course, but it was also a place upon which dreams are based!

In some of the cars, fare list boards were still in position behind the glass panels in the bulkhead downstairs. Also, on the cars that had the 'A' placed after the number on each front dash, I found that the car number above the fare list boards on a panel on the bulk-head next to the ceiling inside the car was, say, 118, not 118A, an omission that was left from 1926/1927 when the English Electric Pivotal cars were delivered from Preston. This memory eluded me altogether until I read about it in Keith Terry's Oldest Cars in Leeds story. The story triggered my memory as: 'Oh! I remember that too'.

Whilst standing with the cars here I remember thinking again how long would it be before these treasures of tramway history would be considered for sale or scrapping. Even if I had known such facts, what could I, a 15 year-old schoolboy, totally biased to tramcars, have done about it? Some of the cars could be bought, no doubt, but where could I put one? We lived in a terrace house in Harehills and my parents could not and would not, under any circumstances, have bought a tramcar, no matter how much their son tried to persuade them.

No, the only answer was to record them thoroughly which Keith Terry did to perfection. I recorded them for posterity from a personal aspect. I felt that they could almost talk to me. Of course, on this day of discovery I had no idea that the details I took and the impressions the cars made on me would surface again in written form fifty six years later. When one is fifteen it's very hard to think of fifty six weeks later, never mind half a century! Now, in 1942 I could fill in the details of the cars in that big gap in my Book when I got home.

That gap of previously unseen cars was not the only gap in the Book. 280 to 282 were still missing, Pivotal car 63 and Horsfield 166 were too. There were quite a few elusive balcony cars in the 300s. 321 and the other two cars in that family of Converts, Beeston Converts 349 and 368, P22 385 and Pivotal 441. All these were gaps. Such gaps that remained in the Hull car series 446 to 477 would be filled as the cars came into service, I could see these any time. The missing Leeds cars could quite easily be in service somewhere in the City but our paths hadn't crossed during school journeys or even depot visits,

I well remember a bike ride to Bramley Depot via Corn Exchange and Armley Road on a particular hunt for 166 and 165. With permission I was allowed to look around the cars and lo! there was 166 with its Crompton West controllers, which I'd heard about but knew nothing about electrically. Discovery of 165 remained for a later date on which I was able to photograph its Maley and Taunton truck and the car in wartime khaki. It was always so exciting to find a 'lost' car.

Hidden corners of K.D. produced some 'lost' cars. 349 for instance had been in the paint shop and possibly other sections of the works as well and eventually emerged in khaki. I can remember thinking when I saw the car: 'Don't the numbers 349 look strange on a khaki background, especially on a Convert. 339, of course, looked equally as strange (Chapter 4). There was a war on and traditions were being usurped of necessity but, I hoped, temporarily.

The discovery of the eight 'A-cars' that were the remains of the separate set of numbered cars and the sixteen consecutively numbered 'magic twos', plus the other balcony cars in the 300s was a major event for me and may be a reason why, over the years, I have had a recurring dream about Leeds cars. The dream occurs in the present day, years after the cars have gone from Leeds. I am standing at the entrance to a tram depot which I do not recognise as being in Leeds. It bears no resemblance to any building in Leeds where cars were shedded. Then I am walking down a slope into the depot and in front of me are various Leeds cars. The last dream included cars 136, 201, 253, 369 and 82, all in Leeds pre-1948 livery. I remember my reaction in the dream as being: 'So this is where all the cars have gone. I knew they couldn't have all been scrapped.' I then come out

Plate 78: Car 165, the only Horsfield or P.35 with a Maley and Taunton Swing Link Truck. This photograph shows the truck in maroon when the car was painted in wartime khaki about January 1943. Author.

of the depot into countryside which I do not recognise and, on asking a person in obvious tramway uniform where this place is, the reply is always: 'near NORWICH'. Leeds cars never die. They remain alive and in service in one's mind.

However, to return to Torre Road Top Shed in 1942. Whilst totally absorbed in the discovery of the 'old cars' I became aware of shouts from a long way off. Not having any worries about trespass I took no notice. I had full permission to be there. On leaving the 'secret' Shed I found that the shouting was from a one-legged man who was down near what appeared to be a watchman's building near the Lupton Avenue entrance to this Top Shed. So, not being a trespasser I walked down to this man who was behaving in an almost demented manner. It was apparent that no amount of explanation would have any effect and he could balance and hop very well on one leg whilst waving his crutch at me. So I finally gave up and returned to the Service Depot through the Bus Garage, much to the man's surprise and waving of the crutch.

Mr Downey said this man was a good watchman who didn't care who he shouted at if he considered trespassers were about. On every subsequent visit I was shouted at by this man, if he saw me!

Not to worry, I had found the secret cars and I was very, very satisfied.

Collecting my bike from the stub track in the Service Depot, I thanked Mr Downey and his colleague for a most rewarding time and rode back home to tell my parents about the little piece of Tramway history that I had uncovered. Once at home and reflecting on the excitement of the discoveries of this day, it struck me that it was such a shame that all these characterful cars should just be left to fade away in rust and dust.

This very personal view does not take note of the practicalities of the day like maintenance problems in wartime, body defects, electrical faults or the rejection by passengers who had been putting up with austere conditions and who were shouting for comfortable new trams like 272 etc. or new buses after the war.

My impressions of these 'old cars' and indeed many of Leeds cars were and are romantic to some degree. Characterful cars, yes! but from a much more personal aspect.

The cars themselves were individuals to me. Even the way they 'looked' at me at the Top Shed was individual. For instance 301, outside on Track 7 (see Plate 68) had a large box for the route number and destination. This car appeared to be looking at me through full-size spectacles, though in this case with misted-over glass. 299 however, only had a destination box and along with the others that had this narrow box, or only the frame, seemed to be looking at me over the top of pince-nez. Almost Dickensian, in fact. The cars inside the shed were lucky, they had not suffered the effects of weather. Those few that were outside were very unkempt and gave me the impression that they had given up the fight for a return to service. They looked tired and sad, their weather-beaten windows and paintwork that was mildewed over looked to me as if they had closed their eyes in resignation to their last trip to Low Fields Road. That would not occur until they had been at Torre Road for another three years, but nobody knew that in 1942.

This then is the story of my first and unforgettable visit to Torre Road Top Shed. During 1942 on another visit to the depot first and then to the Top Shed, I learned that the majority of the 'magic twos' and the 'A-cars' had been taken up to Temple Newsam. One 'A-car', 125A had even been sold - to Rotherham. (Plate 121) I have no memory of going to see the cars on the tracks at Temple Newsam. They were left up there from about mid-1942 to just after May 4th 1943. On this day a head-on collision occurred between Pivotal car 128 and Horsfield 187, a type of accident almost unheard of on Leeds Tramways. Soon after this, all those 'magic twos' and 'A-cars' were brought down again to Torre Road Top Shed.

Some further cars had arrived at the shed during the absence of the cars at Temple Newsam and included the breakdown car 297 (after 25.10.1942) and the last Convert 339 which, by its position at the back of the Shed on Track 4, looked as though it had been put up

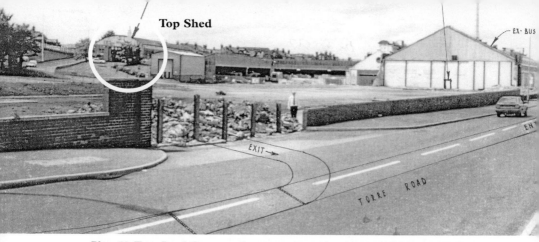

Plate 79: Torre Road Garage and an open space where the tram depot was. The Top Shed can be seen at the top left of the picture on 14 July 1997. Author.

just before the return of the cars from Temple Newsam. Did 297 carry out its last act as breakdown Car by towing faulty 339 to Lupton Avenue and then propelling it into the shed, 297 staying there too? Whatever was the matter with 339 for it to be put up here so soon after entering service and, no doubt, being pronounced fit for service?

The saga of the 'old cars' at Torre Road Top Shed between early 1942 and late 1944 remains with me as an exciting period in my Tramway life. A period which saw my transition from a tramway-orientated schoolboy to a Tramway-employed teenager (Chapter 8).

In hindsight it was as well that I was not in Leeds when those tramway characters were led away from Torre Road. Witnessing their fate would have been heart-rending for me.

After a life of almost 60 years, even the Torre Road tram depot and bus garage, latterly one large bus garage, at Torre Road, came to the end of its transport life in 1996 and in August, 1998, even Torre Road Top Shed was demolished, leaving behind only memories of all the excitements that were to be found in and around the once purpose-built, up-to-date buildings.

Leeds City Tramways Coat of Arms as seen on the side of the car 399 at the National Transport Museum at Crich. Author.

Chapter Seven

CARS OF CHARACTER

Leeds tramcars generally were things, or characters, dependent on one's viewpoint. They were characters to me, even more so after my discovery of the 'old cars' at Torre Road.

They have remained so!

The overall subject and discussion of Leeds tramcars has a calming effect for me nowadays. For instance during the recent prolonged worry and ultimate negotiations of a house sale, the study again and again of the photographs of Leeds cars up to 1945 had a great load-shedding effect until it was necessary to return to present-day problems.

It was during one of these quiet periods that I realised that ever since I got to know Leeds cars, to me the various types had a character of their own. Also the Pivotals, P.22s, P.35s, Converts, etc., had individuals amongst them which were characters themselves.

From the beginning of my observations of Leeds trams, 1933, I had taken note of their colours, dark blue and cream. Later a few cars, the new ones, were painted pale blue and cream. No argument. Those were the colours of Leeds cars. Never mind the buses.

The Leeds Coat of Arms was there, the name of the General Manager was there, the car number in the individual Leeds style was there and the type of destination indicator and its style of lettering of the Route Number, Destination and Via blinds was there too. Even the position of the destination indicator box was an accepted part of Leeds cars. A lot was said about the box obstructing passengers' forward vision from the top deck. Perhaps it did, but like many other things, this could be overcome if an effort was made. What about the coaches on the railways? Impossible to see-out-front on those. Wasn't it nice, however when the Middletons, then 272, 273 and 274 arrived, followed by Converts. Much later, on the railways, when the diesel multiple units came into service and for the very first time passengers could see-out-front without obstruction.

Returning to Leeds cars, all these accepted items were, of course, applied to the cars at Kirkstall Works by L.C.T. staff.. In so doing, the L.C.T. management imparted to the cars considerable pride in their appearance and thus a Leeds character was formed. Their characters seemed to fit with the routes that they were usually on.

In 1943 when I thought I had become familiar with most of Leeds

MIDDLETONS ON ROUNDHAY AND HAREHILLS ROAD							
No.	Date	No.	Date	No.	Date	No	Date
						259,261	
271	15-6-42	259	23-9-42		17-11-43	256	29-1-43
257	16-6-42	269,271 262	24-9-47	263	18-11-43	258	30-1-43
262	18-6-42		25-9-92	270	19-11-43	271	31-1-43
258	19-6-42	265	26-9-42	258 262	20-11-43	258	1-2-43
269	22-6-42	267 269	28-9-42	269	23-11-43	260	2-2-43
264	23-6-42	259	30-9-92	268,270 271	24-11-43	263	3-2-43
271	24-6-42	271,269 261	1-10-42	261 271 256	25-11-43	271	4-2-43
271	25-6-42	263	2-10-92		26-11-43	262	5-2-43
269	26-6-42	256 265,271	3-10-42	270 260 236	27-11-43	262	8-2-43
260	30-6-42	260 256,257	5-10-42	271,268	30-11-43	271	9-2-43
263	1-7-42	262	6-10-42	271,261 268	1-12-43	261	10-2-43
271	2-7-42		7-10-42	269,258	2-12-43	261,271 258	11-2-43
269	7-7-42	256,269	8-10-42	256,264	3-12-43	271,263	12-2-43
256	8-7-42	268,264	9-10-42	269 257,265	4-12-43	270	16-2-43
263	9-7-42	263,257 263,271	12-10-92	263,265 271,259	7-12-43	271 264	17-2-43
262	10-7-42	266 271,258	13-10-42	267 270	8-12-42	257	18-2-43
257	13-7-42	259,269 262,269	16-10-42	256 270	9-12-42	260	19-2-43
271	14-7-42	266	14-10-42	271	11-12-42	258	20-2-43
262	15-7-42	262	15-10-42	260	12-12-42	270 257	21-2-43
271	16-7-42	269 266	19-10-42	268	14-12-42	261 262	22-2-41
270	23-7-42	276	20-10-42	259	15-12-42	257 262	23-2-43
271	24-7-42	266	21-10-42	260	16-12-42		24-2-43
271	5-8-42	271 268	22-10-42	259	19-2-42	262 271 270	25-2-43
263	1-9-42	269	23-10-42	259	23-12-42		2-3-43
262 262	2-9-42	271	24-10-42	267	24-12-42	270	3-3-43
267 269	3-9-42	267	27-10-42	258	29-12-42	264	4-3-43
257	4-9-42	271 276	29-10-42	263	5-1-43	264 270	5-3-43
264 286	5-9-42	266 260,265	30-10-42	256	6-1-43	261	9-3-43
264	7-9-42		2-11-42	264 256,267	7-1-43	262	11-3-43
262 261	8-9-42	255	3-11-42	256,267	8-1-43	261	12-3-43
263,264	9-9-42	269	6-11-42	260,261	12-1-43	271	15-3-43
262	10-9-42	258 267	7-11-42	26c	15-1-43	261	16-3-43
258	15-9-42	263,268 269 264	9-11-42	258	19-1-43	257	17-3-43
261 261	18-9-42		10-11-42	258 260	20-1-43	262	19-3-43
256	17-9-42	269	11-11-42	263	21-1-43	270	23-3-43
266	18-9-42	261 269 256	12-11-42	267,255	26-1-43	267	24-3-43
269	21-9-42		13-11-42	267	27-1-43	270	25-3-43
261	22-9-43	258	16-11-43	262 260	28-1-43	259	26-3-43

Plate 80: On 15 June 1942, I was surprised to see a Middleton car, No. 271 well away from its usual route, travelling up Roundhay Road. The list is from my observations of these cars and shows which cars carried out this service. Middleton cars (see Plate 10) had never before travelled north of Boar Lane. Author.

cars, I realised something about the way I looked at the cars. When any car appeared in view, anywhere on the system, my mind seemed to 'scan' the car, simultaneously registering the car's features and whether the car 'looked right', whether its number, destination, direction of travel, the place I saw it, the location and style of lettering of the destination blinds within their respective box divisions, its truck, its paintwork, its bow, its controllers, its adverts or lack of adverts were in any way different to normal for that car or type of car.

As an example take Horsfield 165. This was the car that had a Maley and Taunton Swing Link truck like 272 and was the only Horsfield so fitted. The car was always based at Bramley Depot. In 1942 or 1943 cars very rarely came off their regular routes, except when travelling to K.D. (possibly via Swinegate Depot) for servicing, or to special events like football or cricket matches.

I saw 165 in Boar Lane en route to the turning loop at the Corn Exchange. I expected to see 14-Corn Exchange up in the front and rear destination boxes and Corn Exchange in the lower saloon boxes, the car having come from Bramley. Simultaneously the overall appearance of the car was appraised, dark blue and cream generally and that all the 'bits and pieces' were in their right places. If all was in order then my attention was rapidly transferred to each of all the other cars that were about and the same appraisal given to each car. Every appraisal would only take a few seconds but if everything was not as expected a note was made to check the car later.

Later I saw 165 in Boar Lane and it had 3-Harehills up and turned left up Briggate. The split-second thought was: 'What's 165 doing off 14 and on 3? For it to be on 3 it must be out of Swinegate Depot, so why the change in routine?' Of course, if 165 hadn't been seen for some time on 14 or any other route one wondered what had happened to it and when it explained its absence by appearing painted in wartime khaki, this really caused eyes to pop, even though it was still on 14 out of Bramley Depot. Weren't the people of Armley, Bramley and Stanningley lucky having a depot-full of the 'very good cars' - the Horsfields - for their continuous use?

Similarly to 165's activities, but in rather an extreme case, I was watching from the front seat upstairs on a car en route from Harehills to Town at 8.00am Monday on 15 June 1942 when I saw car 271, a Middleton car, at Sheepscar with 3-Roundhay via Harehills up, and I was amazed that 271 was in such an unexpected place. I was surprised to find that a Middleton car actually had that destination on the blinds! Such was the familiarity with Leeds trams up to 1945.

By this time two other young persons, Jim Soper and Keith Terry, entirely separately and without knowing that anyone else was interested in Leeds trams, were also assessing the character of the cars according to their own standards, upbringing and preferences. We did this out of interest, nothing official, of course. Far from such a thing! Out of this assessment evolved our own favourite cars. Mine is 400, Keith Terry's is 276 (see Plate 83). Both these cars were characters in their own right.

The cars were always clean and smart but some were cleaner and smarter-looking than others. Their lines of design made them look smarter. For instance, in the classic depot photograph of Stanley Road Depot in 1938 by W.A. Camwell there are seven Pivotal cars on parade side by side. The cars are, from left to right, 84, 105, 27, 424, 20, 132 and 61. Three of these cars, 84, 105 and 132 were built by English Electric and although similar in design to the cars built by Brush or Leeds Tramways, i.e. 27, 20, 60 and 424 respectively, their frontal appearance is different and no matter how clean or newly-painted they were they did not look as smart as the Brush cars or Leeds-built cars. The front shape of the Brush cars, Nos. 1-75 was, to me, smooth in appearance and therefore automatically smart (see Plate 39). The Leeds-built cars i.e. 424 (out of cars 411- 445) were also smoothish in frontal appearance, though with a deeper front frame under the driver's window. Perhaps a little bias has crept in here - 400 was Leeds-built, wasn't it!

The English Electric cars, 76 - 150 always looked as though their roofs had been made separately to the rest of the car and were just that bit too big. 'Never mind', perhaps someone said at Dick, Kerr Works, 'Plonk it on. Those folks at Leeds will never notice the difference.' But some Leeds folk did notice the difference! That difference remained with those folk forever. Thus there were three character traits amongst the Pivotals. I never thought of cars 394 - 398, 401 and 403 - 410 as being Pivotal cars. They were, of course, in that they had Pivotal trucks, but their bodies were of the Beeston variety - a half and half affair?

The individual character amongst the Pivotals was Brush car 44 because it had transverse seats inside. This car fairly oozed superiority over its stablemates especially when on Lawnswood. Not to be outdone, English Electric car 89 was fitted with transverse seats inside, but because of its roof-lid it wasn't quite up to 44's act. I never found out why 44 and 89 were given transverse seats. Again, I probably never thought to ask! Cars 82 and 87 had 'doors on', but even this did not compensate for their roof-lids. There was also car 111 - 'Lord Nelson'.

The Pivotal cars with Beeston-type bodies, 394 - 398 etc. never quite made the 'smooth and smart' parade. They were built by Leeds Tramways a bit later than the Beeston cars but their appearance head-on was different. Perhaps because they had Pivotal trucks they looked that bit taller than the Beeston cars, but that was only an impression. Also, head-on the top deck seemed to be a little wider than the bottom deck and thus the smoothness in appearance was lost. They were easily distinguishable in side-view from the Beeston cars, even if their wheels were obscured from view by a fence or motor vehicle.

The old soldiers of the fleet, the experienced travellers, as it were, were the P.22s or Beeston cars. These cars, though ageing, were a dignified lot. (370 - 388, 390 - 393, 399 and 402).

They appeared to me to sit the rails in a determined manner. They were capable cars and seemed to say that they knew it. To me they said, 'We can go anywhere on the system and no matter what the conditions or weather, we will succeed!'

They did not have doors-on and, generally, were not smooth and smart cars but the treatment given to 399 at Crich when the car was 65 years old shows what the others could have looked like, even in dark blue and cream.

There were no individual characters in this group of cars. 370-375 seemed to try to hide their drivers from passengers' view - they had their stairs going up the opposite way. Car 389, though not a character really, did not have air brakes and although a Beeston car in appearance never went on Beeston, but nevertheless it was always let-go at Harehills Corner.

There was no doubt that the real characters of the fleet were the old-timers, the remaining 'empty-top-ends' cars or Balcony cars. They were the 'A-cars', whose numbers were 115A, 117A, 118A and 120A - 123A and 125A, the 'magic twos' and the rest whose numbers were 283 to 299 and 300 to 320, 322 to 331, 333 to 338 and 342, respectively. These cars were built by Leeds Tramways between 1908 and 1919 and had the looks of Edwardian ladies, especially the 'A-cars'. The vestibules that were added to these 'A-cars' just before the Great War did not quite match the original shape of their bodies. They seemed to billow at each end giving them a certain dignity not apparent in the rest of the Balcony cars, as I found on 118A. (Chapter 6) (See Plate 121)

Perhaps a not unfair impression was transmitted to me by these cars when in service and could be described thus; 'When the weather was good the Balcony cars were very, very good, but when the weather was bad were horrid.' Nevertheless these cars were (and still are) revered by myself as part of Leeds Tramways past. They had plenty of spirit left even though they were already 25 years old when I first became fully aware of them. They had been through the Great War and were about to give service through the Second World War. By 1945 when most of them were scrapped at Low Fields Road they were 35 years old. There are a considerable number of photographs of the Balcony cars around (though not many of the 'A-cars' in service). I hope these photographs will be treasured.

The smooth and smart cars were the P.35s or Horsfields (151 to 254). They knew it. They looked after their drivers and: 'We close our doors, you know. We look after our passengers' comfort and we have push-bells, not rubbishy cords. Our bells sound like 'thang-thang' not 'thack-thack' or 'ting-ting.' We don't clatter the stair-covers down either and most important of all we can stop with at least four types of brakes. We are the 'very model of a modern Leeds tramcar' (with apologies to Gilbert and Sullivan)

The P.35s could go on any route, like the P.22s did and could be depended upon for a good performance. Cars 158, 165 and 166 were the specialists amongst the Horsfields. (See Chapter 1)

But then appeared 255 and the rest of the Middleton cars. They had W Vane Morland stamped all over them. 255, their leader, soaked up all the attention given to these very long, very smooth and exceptionally smart cars. I think that they were the best cars in the world!

They said to me in a most dignified fashion over their double bumpers:- 'We have been made especially for Middleton - nowhere else. We shall never travel on other routes, north of the River Aire.' These gliding cars for Middleton had two headlamps each end, they allowed their passengers a clear view to see-out-front upstairs and were painted light-blue and cream. They made their own noise on the tracks with their bogies.

'We give our drivers a seat in his own cabin. We are very fast and comfortable cars,' they could almost be heard to say this as they came out of Swinegate Depot into Swinegate and into service.

The individual among the Middletons (Nos. 255 to 271) was 255. This was the General Manager's car. Unfortunately it was taken off 12-Middleton and relegated to 25-Hunslet. Not the proper place for such an up-to-date and characterful car.

After 255, there were sixteen Middleton cars, eight built by Brush at Loughborough (256 - 263) and eight by English Electric at Preston (264-271). It was always possible to distinguish between a Brush Middleton car and an English Electric Middleton car from either the front or side, in the same way as I could distinguish between a Brush Pivotal car and an English Electric Pivotal car. I always felt that the Brush Middletons looked that bit neater, head-on, than did the English Electric Middletons. Window treatment was the main reason, I remember. Looking at the cars at right angles, the main difference was in the style of the lower saloon ventilators. The style and appearance of these cars compares very favourably with the double-deck buses of modern design. Not bad at all for a 1934 design. (See page 191)

Immediately after the Middletons, almost as a makepeace, 272 appeared, followed by 273 and 274 (See Chapter 1). These three cars were smaller versions of the Middletons and only had four wheels. They were made for Lawnswood, Moortown and Roundhay routes. They too looked after their drivers and passengers, but were rather clumsy towards their conductors and, along with the Middleton cars, had 'doors-on'. They were comfortable but haughty cars and they seemed to 'know' that Lawnswood and Roundhay were their 'patch'. I always felt that they didn't want to speak to me.

Nevertheless, they were comfortable cars and were waited for by a lot of intending passengers who let-go other cars in order to have a comfortable journey. I remember that if we were able to travel to Roundhay Park from Harehills on any of these three cars, it was always such a pleasure to sit upstairs and see-out-front up the reserved tracks to Oakwood and Roundhay.

If each of these cars had been given a name, 272 might have been

Plate 81: Car 277 at Briggate Barriers in 1943. The car was one of three that came from London in 1939 which were painted in the Middleton-type blue and cream. Author.

named 'Roundhay', 273 'Moortown' and 274 'Lawnswood'.

Then there were the three newcomers from London, the first foreign cars to be brought to Leeds. They were referred to as HR2s and it was not until much later that I found out that the HR part of their type number stood for 'Hilly Route.' They were 277, 278 and 279 and I always referred to them by their number. To me they were important because they came from London, implying that anything 'London' in those days would be most acceptable.

These HR2s were rugged cars, I suppose they had to be to withstand the road and traffic conditions in London. In Leeds, however, they were entirely on their own, rather like evacuees at the beginning of the war and they never appeared to settle down in their northern city. They were heavy and in some ways gaunt in appearance, though the pale-blue Middleton-type paint appeared to soften them a little. Exciting to ride on though, for me, especially when 277 was improved during the war and it then ran on our routes, i.e. Roundhay, Moortown and Lawnswood.

Their character was dull in comparison to, say, the Horsfields. They seemed to me to not want to respond to the handling by Leeds drivers, nor were they very happy about their lack of centre 'shoes' or their new bow-collector 'hat'. They wouldn't behave themselves when stopping as though telling Leeds drivers,

> *'We stop only with the magnetic brake, none of this brake-handle business. We had to stop like that in London, the traffic was so dense'.*

Notwithstanding an apparent dullness or heaviness, I would always be glad to see 277 coming round from Harehills Corner and would get on and try to get to the front upstairs and be reminded of 400's window below the route number box. In fact once or twice on a Saturday, after I started work at Tramways, if 277 was observed to be about in Harehills or if I could find out from either Swinegate or Headingley depots when the car would be at Harehills en route for Roundhay, then I would ride on it right round to Moortown and back to Town, hopefully sitting at the top front all the way. 277 was the better car, after modifications, than the other two.

Then there were the double-characters! The Converts! Now these cars were old soldiers in the new army of Leeds trams. They were built in Leeds about five or six years before I was. Balcony cars then, they were re-built when I was ten years old into very acceptable 'waterproof' cars. So acceptable that at eight o'clock on the morning journey into Town from 1943 onwards instead of the P.22 usually on 5-Beeston at that time (see Chapter 8), I would be able to sit forward-facing and see-out-front upstairs, the anti-blast netting ignored by the pleasure of such a seat. All these cars had doors on and their stairs were straighter and easier for older folk.

The cars so converted were 332, 340, 341, 343 to 369. 339 of course, was my 'surprise' car in 1942. (see Chapter 4).

They all were smoothed-over characters to me. Their hidden background was immediate post-Great War and therefore they had a kinship with the cars I had found at Torre Road Top Shed, at the same time they had an up-to-date kinship with the Horsfields, (doors-on and stairs) and a little bit of Middleton car had rubbed off on the position of the destination indicator box. The cars that had P22 trucks were akin to the Beeston cars and those that had Hurst Nelson trucks were akin to the 'old cars'.

So these cars were a right mixture. They did not, in my eyes, allow this historical mixture to influence their characters. What did have an effect was the fact that because of brake equipment, some Converts could travel on any route, and some were prohibited from the Beeston route. I gave the name 'Beeston Convert' to those so allowed. The remainder I called 'non-Beeston Converts'. Beeston Convert numbers were 332, 346, 347, 349, 350, 354 - 359, 361 - 369. The others were 340, 341, 343 - 345, 348, 351 - 353 and 360 and, in 1942, 339. As I have said in Chapter 3 the Beeston Converts seemed to sit the road better than their non-Beeston colleagues. Perhaps this was due to the different trucks. I could always tell a Beeston Convert, even in the blackout, not by its travelling sound but by its braking sound. They seemed to slurr-r-r when stopping. They were very capable cars, rather like the Beeston 370's and could be found on other routes as fill-ins as required.

Plate 82: Car 275 was converted from balcony car 119A in 1938 and along with 276 (Plate 83) and 321 formed a distinctive family of three. The car was photographed at Easterly Road, Harehills in 1943. Author.

On older, pre-war photographs, they, along with the non-Beeston Converts, could be identified at once because of the cream band, like the Middletons, below the top deck windows. This cream band disappeared by the beginning of the war. I was sorry to see a distinguishing mark go. The cars were a little chip off the Middleton block.

The non-Beeston Converts were totally different in ride-characteristics. They bounced and flounced. Although the same body alterations were carried out, this bouncing took the edge off body improvements. It was almost as though they were saying to me: 'We wish they hadn't given us this heavy rucksack to carry. Our 'boots' were not made for heavy load-carrying and we sometimes feel top-heavy and then bounce over joints'.

Towards the end of their life, this continuous extra load-carrying showed itself on both types of Converts by the drooping of the body

Plate 83: Car 276 photographed at Low Fields Road in 1943. The car was converted from balcony car 124A and is seen here after a repaint in wartime in blue and cream, not khaki. The destination blind, put up specially, was highly optimistic. Author.

ends. They seemed to be crying out for support!

There were three other cars, all Converts, that were very 'Special Cars'. Two of them I had not seen and the other I had neither seen nor knew about. They were gaps in my Book, long after finding most of the other cars in the fleet. By 1943, I had discovered these cars and what a surprise they were.

Car numbers 275, 276 and 321 really were characters in their own right. Their history made them so, apart from their looks. Research by Keith Terry and others has shown that the three cars were converted from the 'A-cars', no less! Which explains why, once I had found the 'A-cars' at Torre Road and then eventually saw them in service, there was, I thought, a similarity of shape in the vestibules. Only an impression of similarity, but that impression has stayed with me over the years. These cars were all different in various ways. Keith Terry describes their history in his article 'Some Early Memories of the Oldest Trams in Leeds during the last War', which finally confirmed and added to the bare facts.

But, when I found the cars, I took them as they were on the streets and characterised them without knowing their origins. 275 and 276 struck me as being modernised 'magic two's. They were obviously very different from the other Converts. 275 looked to me to be a haughty car and almost gave me the impression of being the 'son' of 321. In this instance 321 was not the older car, however. 275 having air-track brakes, had most of the space under the side panels down to the rails taken up with mechanical equipment. I wasn't an engineering draughtsman when I observed these cars so my description is as a layman. Car 276, because of its Hurst Nelson truck and no air-brakes of any kind gave me the impression of femininity - its 'skirts' seemed to be longer than the other cars. Treatment of its window-bases on the dashes also improved its vestibules and accentuated its lady-like appearance. The car was not allowed on the Beeston routes. 321 and 275 were converted from 116A and 119A respectively, and were allowed on the Beeston routes.

I felt then - and still do - that 321 and 276 were 'parents' and their son was 275. There was no doubt that they were an individual family of three cars, designed very much like a Horsfield with flush bottom deck sides and like the other Converts elsewhere. Their top-deck frontal treatment was individual and they could be recognised easily from any angle, any distance. I wondered if Mr Daggett at K.D. had a hand in their 'design and build' routines? After I had left Leeds, I heard that the three cars had been re-numbered for certain practical reasons, but they will always be 275, 276 and 321 in my memory. Without any mourning this family had died by 1951.

However, historical facts sometimes appear out of the blue and the history of 276 has proved no exception. On March 1st, 1995 by courtesy of Keith Terry, I learnt that in 1924 when 276 was 124 (not 124A) an experimental Pivotal truck was fitted to the car. A Balcony car without, then with, driver's vestibules then, with a Pivotal truck, albeit temporarily. I can't imagine a Pivotal truck under a Balcony car.

The car soldiered on, becoming 124A in 1926/ 1927, for another fourteen years. It was, no doubt, seen by myself in Harehills and accepted as part of the system, until 1938 when it returned to K.D. for a complete rebuild. In the re-design the destination and route number indicators were positioned in the same place as on the Middleton cars and indeed as on all the other Converts. The panel below the top deck windows became cream, again as on the Middletons and the panels below the lower deck windows were straightened in the fashion of the Horsfields. The car then took the number 276, from one of the 'old cars' recently scrapped, thus becoming an individual car within the family of three. 276 had been part-Pivotal, part-Balcony car and had become part-Horsfield, part-Middleton in its conversion to a fully enclosed car. Even its number changed four times. Built in K.D. as 124, the car became 124A, then 276 and finally 342. With a history like that and a very pleasing final lady-like appearance, perhaps the car could be allowed to change its 'mind' so many times!?

Wouldn't it be fascinating to hear about all the thinking and planning that went into this car's history over the forty years. Thinking back in time from a comfortable existence in 1999, it would be an adventure in tramways to return to about 1923 and stand in the Works Superintendent's office at K.D. for the next 30 years and listen to the repair, maintenance and design programmes for the existing and for new cars, always provided that one could return to 1999. What a history that would have produced, so long as people recorded what they saw. Oh well, one can occasionally dream, surely?

Another thought on character indication on Leeds cars was provided by whoever arranged the contracts for advertisements for the cars and for those advertisements to be applied to the cars. It was where those adverts were placed on the top half of the cars that created the impression of a car that was not easily forgotten. I have already mentioned the 'Pontings' advert on car 400 (Chapter 1). Another car (of many) that had distinctive adverts on each end was 241. The typically-Leeds advert on the cars was for 'Melbourne Ales', placed along the sides and on the ends on many cars. 241, a Horsfield, had the only short advert for 'Melbourne Ales' on each end. There was a larger space, when viewed head-on, between each end of the advert and the edge of the car. Thus 241 was instantly

Plate 84: Car 201 - a Horsfield or P.35 painted overall for National Pedestrian Crossing Week in 1949. Courtesy Frank Graves.

identifiable in head-on view, before its number could be seen. It was a car that was livened up by an advert, because its paintwork always appeared to be dull. The 'Melbourne Ales' advert on the front of a Horsfield (P.35) always made me think that the car was 'smiling' at me.

Car 360, a non-Beeston Convert, copied London Transport buses in placing an advert for 'Picture Post' on each side of the destination indicator box, looking like a pair of eyes.

A question! Which section of Leeds Tramways dealt with the allocation of advertisements to be applied to trams?

Leeds Tramways occasionally used their cars for publicity purposes in addition to normal advertising from 1909 onwards. The well-known photographs of 119 and 120, when brand new at the opening of the Rawdon route and the Recruiting Car of 1914 are typical examples. It would be very interesting to know if there were decorated cars for the Silver Jubilee of King George V in 1935 and for the Coronation of King George VI in 1937. Which car was decorated for the opening of the Civic Hall in 1933? My memory fails me on such possible cars. In 1942 Horsfield 230 was painted in wartime khaki and then was decorated overall for a 'Safety First' Exhibition in November 1945. The Second World War put a stop to 'decorated' cars, as they were then called and it was not until April 7-14, 1949 that Horsfield 201 was painted overall to draw attention to National Pedestrian Crossing Week. On March 25th, 1950, car 309, the only Balcony car left, was decorated overall for National Children's Safety Week. After the drabness of the war years these three cars made a great impression when they appeared on the streets. On the front of each destination indicator of both cars 201 and 309 was a large photograph of a Leeds policeman pointing at 'you' in the manner of the famous poster of the Great War showing Lord Kitchener pointing at 'you' and saying 'Your country needs you!' The policeman on cars 201 and 309 was P.C. 647 Reuben Graves who was once described as the 'best known and most photographed man in the Leeds Police Force'. The photograph of 201 was given to me in 1995 by Mr Frank Graves, the son of P.C. 647.

Car 359, one of the Beeston Converts was, I think, one of the last cars to be treated overall, in this case with an advertisement for National Savings from 1951 for a year or two.

It must be fairly obvious that all Leeds cars appeared characterful to me. The very fact that I am writing about them over 50 years after living with them - and writing about them as though they are still 'alive'- says everything about the impression the trams gave me.

Chapter Eight

A Job Amongst the Trams

Even in wartime there were opportunities to be taken. During the period May to August, 1943 there occurred some of the most exciting, anxious and rewarding happenings of my parallel lives, i.e. those of school and tramways. In hindsight the object of both these lives was to work to bring them into one at Leeds Tramways.

Between the day of the accident at Temple Newsam on 4 May 1943 and the School Certificate Examinations, events took place rapidly which were to actually bring these two lives together at Leeds Tramways.

On 24 May, one year and one month after Mother wrote on my behalf to Mr W. Vane Morland (Chapter 5), a form arrived from the Establishments Officer at Civic Hall. The form had the magnificent title of :-

---

City of Leeds

WAR-TIME SCHEME FOR SELECTION BY INTERVIEW OF CANDIDATES APPLYING FOR JUNIOR APPOINTMENTS ON THE STAFF OF THE CORPORATION

Plate 85: A copy of the actual lengthy heading of a form I had to complete in 1943. Author.

The form was filled in and returned with references to a very well-known name at that time, O.A. Radley, Town Clerk at the Civic Hall. Mr Radley was also Establishments Officer. Explanatory notes supplied with the form described the Scheme and required amongst other details that the parents of applicants were to have 'been resident in the City for not less than twelve months!' On 23 June, a Roneo-ed letter arrived from the Establishment Officer requiring me to 'attend for interview at the Education Offices in Calverley Street on 8 July at 8.00pm.'

During this last month we all had been swotting hard in preparation for the examinations but on journeys to and from school I still kept my eyes open both on and for any trams. I dared not take time off from schoolwork revision to go tram-hunting. Examination

Plate 86: Cars 187 and 128 after their head-on collision on the Temple Newsam route on 4 May 1943 (see Plate 93). Yorkshire Post.

worries were foremost and I was more worried than some because I found Mathematics difficult. History, Geography, English and Chemistry would not be of much use in Leeds Tramways, I thought. It turned out that Maths would be the least of my worries there. This period for a 16 year-old was most bewildering because on June 30th my mother had written, again on my behalf, to Mr W. Vane Morland with the result that on 6 July, two days before I was to be interviewed at Calverley Street, a letter arrived from Leeds City Transport, rubber-stamped by Mr W. Vane Morland, initialled by the General Manager's Secretary but written by Mr T. Ellis, Constructional Engineer. The letter said,

'Please ask your son to call and see our Mr Ellis, Constructional Engineer, at Head Office, Swinegate on Saturday, July 10th instant at 10.00am.'

Apparently Heads of Departments did not write directly to possible future junior employees in those days.

So here I had two interviews in two days and though both were for possible employment in Corporation Departments, there was no connection between the interviews. Obviously the interview at Tramways was the important one. The interview at Calverley Street was conducted by no less a person than Mr George Guest, Director of Education for Leeds. With him in a semicircle, of which I was the hub, were five other gentlemen and one lady. Imagine that nowadys and at eight o'clock at night too!

Before any result of this interview could be known the interview at Tramways took place. This appointment meant that I would have to enter the Tramways Head Office across the road from Swinegate Depot; as Jim Wade had presumed, Oooh! I would have a letter with me to prove my appointment and as a young lad I would not be chased out: in any case I would have Mother with me and let anyone try and be offhand to her.

Now, all staff in Corporation Service worked on Saturday mornings at that time, but were allowed to wear a sports coat and flannels and collar and tie, of course, but not necessarily a suit. Nevertheless, suit on for me, even on a Saturday and down to Harehills Corner for a 5-Beeston car to Town. Yes, it was going down Vicar Lane to Corn Exchange but we stayed on the car to Watson Cairns in Lower Briggate in order to walk down to Swinegate without having to dodge the traffic at Boar Lane/Briggate Junction and risk any splashing or marks on our clothes. My mother came too because she was asked to do so!

Head Office had what appeared to be marble steps and two substantial centre hand-rails leading up to a revolving door behind which was a reception desk from where we were taken up in the lift to the second floor, again a marble tiled surface with three imposing doors facing on to this landing. Two other swing doors, one on each side of the lift and stairwell, were part of wood partitions leading to separate corridors. The wood was polished mahogany. We were suitably impressed as we were meant to be and I thought that I would have to be on best behaviour if I was lucky enough to come to work here. A bit different to school corridors and a Headmaster's study woodwork.

We were shown to Mr Ellis's office - through the right-hand swing door and through his mahogany door. Mr Ellis was dapperly-dressed and he welcomed us in a human way and put us at ease at once. At least, he thought he put me at ease, for how can a young lad, being interviewed for a job he really wants, be at ease in front of a Head of Department and for whom he hoped he would be working in a most junior position?

I was told in no uncertain terms that 'hard work would be necessary to be successful in the Department' and that 'the first step will be to obtain the School Certificate'. I groaned to myself, thinking about Maths! As I remember, nothing was asked about my knowledge, if any, of Leeds Tramcars. Then Mr Ellis interviewed my mother, on her own. Five days later on 15 July a letter from the Establishment Officer at the Civic Hall arrived to tell me that, 'Your name has been placed on the 'Approved list of Candidates for Junior Appointments in the Corporation Service.' Even then, it seems, one hand of an official body did not know what the fingers of the other hand were doing! My interview with Mr Ellis had nothing to do with the 'Approved List.' So, between 4 May and 5 August, 1943 the following ten major events - they were major for me - made this time very exciting but very worrying, not made any easier by the cloud of the exams hanging over me:

1. 4 May: Collision between cars 128 and 187 at Temple Newsam.
2. 8 May: An investigative visit to K.D. to see cars 128 and 187.
3. 24 May: Form arrived for Junior Candidates to Corporation Staff.
4. 23 June: Letter from Town Clerk re. interview at Calverley Street.
5. School Certificate Examinations about now.
6. 30 June: Letter on my behalf from Mother to W Vane Morland.
7. 5 July: Letter from W. Vane Morland re. interview on 10 July.
8. 8 July: Interview by Director of Education.
9. 10 July: Interview at Leeds City Transport.
10. 15 July: Letter from Town Clerk - on 'Approved List'.

It was not possible to deduce the outcome of the interview with Mr Ellis - it never is on the jobs one really wants! So for three weeks my parents and I worried and worried, because I had now left Cockburn High School (with no regrets at all.) and we were wondering if I had a job on Leeds City Transport or even in the Corporation.

And then No.11 - a letter arrived dated 5 August, addressed to me this time - typed address, daren't open it - the letter said:- 'I have decided to offer you a temporary appointment in the Drawing Office. Please report for duty on Monday, 6 September, 1943 at 8.30am.' Whoopee! It was signed by the General Manager.

Can you imagine how I felt? After all the years of interest in Leeds trams and all the preparations like getting to know Leeds, the tram and bus routes, the depots etc. but particularly the tramcars, here was my ambition to work 'amongst the trams' achieved, or so I thought. It was wartime, of course and things were severely curtailed, but l was fortunate. l had a job that meant l was going to work at Tramways all the time and not just out of school hours.

When this letter arrived at home we had all sat for the School Certificate Examinations, albeit in my case with great unease, which proved correct because I heard that I had failed mine by one subject,

Plate 87: A copy of the letter of 5 August 1943, offering me a job in Leeds Tramways. An exciting day! Author.

TELEPHONE: CENTRAL 21601.

ALL COMMUNICATIONS TO BE ADDRESSED TO "THE GENERAL MANAGER."

TELEGRAMS "TRAMWAYS, LEEDS.

LEEDS CITY TRANSPORT DEPARTMENT

W. VANE MORLAND, M.I.MECH.E., M.I.A.E. M.INST.T., F.R.S.A. GENERAL MANAGER & CHIEF ENGINEER.

SWINEGATE, LEEDS, 1. 5th August, 1943.

REFERENCE CEG

Mr.G.B. Render,
22 Milan Road,
Leeds.8.

Dear Mr.Render,

With reference to your interview with our Mr.Ellis (Constructional Engineer), I have decided to offer you a temporary appointment in the Drawing Office. I shall be glad, therefore, if you will report for duty on Monday, September 6th, 1943, at 8.30a.m.

Yours faithfully,

W Vane Morland

General Manager.

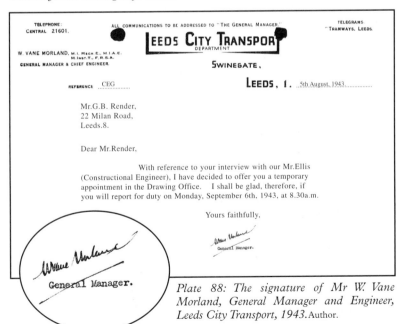

Plate 88: The signature of Mr W. Vane Morland, General Manager and Engineer, Leeds City Transport, 1943. Author.

Maths. However, fate was kind, I had a 'job in the place I wanted but, most luckily for me, Leeds City Transport did not say 'NO' when I told them of my failure.

There were two people on Tramways whom it was necessary to thank for their help and advice. Mr Wade at Swinegate Depot who first made me aware of 'across the road' at Head Office and Mr Daggett at K. D. who first mentioned the 'Drawing Office at Head Office'. I was very pleased to thank them each personally, soon after starting work. I well remember the first day of work at the Transport Department. My parents were just as excited as I was. Up early in order to have a good breakfast, before walking down to Harehills Corner to join all the other folk going to Town at 7.50am. I was allowing myself plenty of time on my first morning. When the first car came along from the Clock Buildings (I don't remember which car but it had to be a car going to Briggate.) I got on and I remember thinking that I was going to work for the Body who operates this car and in the same building as the man whose name I had seen on all the cars, Mr W. Vane Morland. A most exciting and at the same time an unnerving thought.

Getting off the car at the Barriers at Briggate I walked down to Boar Lane/ Briggate Junction, taking in all the tram activity, across to Lower Briggate, and down under the railway bridge to 'this' side of Swinegate. Look in the Depot entrance from a distance and then cross Swinegate to the 'marble steps' of Head Office which was on the corner of Swinegate and Concordia Street.

Now, take a deep breath and up the steps, through the revolving doors to the desk on the left of the doors. Bob took me to the lift and we rode up to the second floor again. (I never found out Bob's

Plate 89: The entrance to the Head Office of Leeds City Transport, Swinegate about 1952. Leeds City Transport/West Yorkshire Archives Service, Wakefield.

Plate 90: Bob at the lift-gates inside the main entrance to Leeds City Transport Head Office. The date could be any time between 1943 and 1960. Leeds City Transport/West Yorkshire Archives Service, Wakefield.

Plate 91: The Mahogany corridor to the Engineering Department leading to the Drawing Office on the second floor of Leeds City Transport Head Office. This view confronted me on my first day at work here on 6 September 1943. Leeds City Transport/West Yorkshire Archives Service, Wakefield.

surname - he was Bob to everybody.) The sounds of the lift control handle and the rattle of the lift gates as they opened or closed stays with me.

Once through the single swing-door next to Mr Ellis's office we walked along a corridor with three mahogany doors on the left and three on the right with one glass door emergency exit to iron steps to the ground. Even the floor was mahogany-coloured, highly-polished linoleum. The corridor was about six feet wide with a ceiling height of ten feet.

At the end of the corridor I was shown by Bob, who was in the uniform of the platform staff, through another mahogany door and he then left me to it. This door had frosted glass panels in its top half and, with a distinctive noise, opened into a rectangular reception cubicle, as wide as the corridor, but with frosted-glass panels from waist height up to about eight feet high. There was no ceiling to this cubicle, presumably so that visitors to the Drawing Office could be heard entering and be attended to quickly.

A vertically-opening, wood-framed glass panel with a brass finger-hold was opposite the door to the corridor and a bell-push was by the side of the panel. When I pressed the bell-push, the panel was immediately pushed up by a well-dressed gentleman who, when I said my name, came around to the side door on the right of the cubicle, shook hands and introduced himself as Mr A.R. Bedell,

Chief Draughtsman. (I would have that designation one day, sixteen years into the future) It was 8.20am and I was early! A good point to me so far, but within minutes that good point was cancelled out. Mr Bedell showed me to a drawing board which was on top of a very long work-top under which were numerous sets of drawers. I had never been in the Drawing Office before, not even at the time of my interview with Mr Ellis. However, looking around I saw nine drawing boards in this very spacious office and within the next few minutes each one was occupied by a man - no noise, no speech, come in, sit down and take stock. (My first split-second impressions.) A high wooden stool was required to sit at any of these drawing boards. The Drawing Office was the width of and on the curved corner of the building at the junction of Swinegate and Leeds Bridge, where 255 came round in November, 1942. Large windows with small panes gave views up Lower Briggate and a plan view of Lower Briggate/Swinegate/Call Lane/Bridge End junction. If one dared to look up from the drawing board, there was a level view to the top of the L.N.E.R. railway bridge over Lower Briggate. Locomotives of the 'Hunt' class were often seen from these windows during my time with Tramways.

I remember, to my chagrin, that on this drawing board on which the board sloped slightly from back to front and was to be mine for a time, were two photographs of trams which I thought may have been put there for my interest, to break the strange ice, as it were. So I picked them up and was about to talk to Mr Bedell about them when he almost shouted at me, 'Put those down. They're not yours!'

That was a good start to a new job, I thought, suitably chastened and having had the early-arrival good point well and truly cancelled out.

Now, it was very apparent to me that a totally new way of life was starting for me. The discipline at Cockburn High School, though strict, was nothing like the strictness and standards that I found I had to adhere to in this Drawing Office. An office and a 'job amongst the trams?' Well, we shall see, I thought.

Within an hour or two of entering Head Office this day, I realised that I had joined a very disciplined routine in an office where juniors were juniors and that was to be remembered, or else! I was introduced to Mr This and Mr That. They all had to be referred to, or addressed as Mister Blakeborough, say. I was told to write down each person's name who worked in the Drawing Office, his title in the office and where he was on the Family Tree of the Engineering Department, all so that I should know everybody quickly.

The first week of my working career flashed by and at its end I was rewarded with my first ever wages - one pound, two shillings and three pence - obtained on presentation of my brass check disc Number 97.

Working amongst what trams? I was not allowed to even look out of a window, never mind tramcars and numbers and routes.

I thought I knew (I knew I knew) a thing or two about Leeds trams, but now I had come to work for the Department that actually operated the cars (and buses too, of course) I found that, in a very quick time, I was deemed to have NO KNOWLEDGE whatever about the System until I had learnt to address staff correctly, how to fetch tea correctly and, long term, how to form letters and figures correctly in pencil and in drawing ink on tracing paper and tracing cloth in order not to ruin a drawing by uneducated lettering.

It took me some time to realise that the assumption that I did not know anything about Leeds trams, was a manifestation of the official attitude towards enthusiasts or V.I.P.s (Very Interested Persons). I remember thinking that I would have to keep my own counsel and watch my step in this office or I'm going to find problems when I go to K.D. or Swinegate Depot, etc.

However, I very soon learnt about the subject matter dealt with in this Drawing Office and obviously life here, though strict, was going to be very, very interesting. All aspects of tramcars, including the Austerity Car 104, which I knew about but was deemed not to know about; all aspects of buses, depots, garages, other buildings, overhead line details, electrical work for everything, planning procedures, forward planning for a tram or bus future after the war and most

Plate 92: The remains of the Drawing Office in the Head Office of Leeds City Transport, seen on 20 June 1997 with ghost drawing boards, etc. superimposed. Courtesy Wetherall, Green & Smith, Leeds.

Plate 93: Car 187 at the Clock Cinema, Easterly Road, newly painted and repaired after the accident at Temple Newsam, Plate 86. Painted in blue and cream but still with white fenders and headlamp masks. No anti-blast netting. August 1943. Author.

interesting of all, permanent way maintenance and renewal.

I was even taught how to photograph things L.C.T. One of the photographs that I received instruction how to take was Horsfield car 223 in wartime khaki at Bramley Town End, outside Bramley Depot. This would be late 1943 or early 1944. How the world changes over 50 years! In May 1995, the firm Exclusive First Editions, model bus and tram manufacturers, brought out an excellent model of 223 based on this very photograph. E.F.E. also produce other excellent models of Horsfield cars in the red livery.

On top of all this was the overall subject of Drawing Office Practice - a very strict, very painstaking subject requiring great concentration and determination to become even a mediocre printer of lettering. The actual drawing wasn't so bad but the problem of joining lines drawn in ink and being able to say: 'You can't see the join, can you?' took a very long time.

The instrument used for drawing lines in ink of any thickness was the ruling pen which was a bone or ivory or black-steel rod about 3 inches long and serrated to give finger grip. One end of this rod was internally threaded to take the solid part of the two chromium-plated, pointed blades. These blades were sprung against a knurled screw, thus giving the facility for thick or very thin lines. There were, of course, different qualities of the steel blades, the finer the steel, the finer the line drawn.

The same ink as that used for lettering was inserted between the blades by the same quill-pointed, squeezable filler. Then it was up to the draughtsman to get to 'know his pen' and to practise hard so that he could produce a drawing where the joins between curved and straight lines could not even be guessed at. There were no such things as Rapidographs then and computer-derived drawings were so much science-fiction.

All this amounted to a thorough engineering draughtsman's apprenticeship and training. They, that is, those persons already in the Drawing Office, were very good teachers, so much so that fifty years later I am still drawing and printing to their high standard. (Well, almost.)

Another boy about my own age, 16 years and 9 months, Ronnie Griffiths, started in the Drawing Office about the same time as I did and as his father was a tram-driver, we learnt about trams and buses from other aspects. We also found that we had the same tastes in music so all in all we got along very well. This was a bonus because the processes that we had to learn in the daily and weekly routines in the Drawing Office had to be done strictly to time and once we were

Plate 94: Car 223 at Bramley Town End. This photograph was the result of a training exercise in photography for me under L.C.T. instruction. 1943/1944. Leeds City Transport.

familiar with things we were able to think 'round corners' for each other which made life so much more pleasant. We were taken about the system by the various staff using public transport because nobody had cars in those days, there was no petrol anyway - and we were expected to 'hear all, see all and say nowt' and learn fast.

At lunch-times or in the dinner hour as we knew it then, that is when I had the chance to go across to Swingate Depot. It was necessary to be introduced before we could visit Sovereign Street Permanent Way Yard. Now I was on the Department, it was possible to talk a lot easier to Mr Wade or Mr Howells or to any of the yard staff in the depot. We were even instructed, sometimes, to go across to the depot to take or fetch - run errands would be a better description I think. Of course I used these times to observe anything out of the ordinary in the depot, especially on tracks 16 to 30 or even just to stand and look!

One thing that was demanded of Ronnie and I was that each morning, as soon as we had carried out the daily preparation duties we had to settle down on our drawing boards under tight supervision for a minimum of three quarters of an hour to practise printing, i.e. learning to form letters, figures, dimensions, fractions, etc., in pencil and in drawing ink using only PEN NIBS. There were no such things as biros or felt-tip pens in those days. The same practice applied immediately after the return from the dinner hour. It was, nevertheless, quite some time before we were sufficiently taught and had reached a level of capability so that we were able to produce any form of drawing at all.

During excursions to various parts of the system with other members of the staff, places that had been secret to me were uncovered including the place that I had seen on my first journey across Leeds Bridge in 1940, i.e. Sovereign Street Yard, where we were eventually introduced. Other secret places were Bramley Depot and Donisthorpe Street Bus Maintenance Works, which was hidden away off Hunslet Road. We went to places like Copley Hill Rectifier Substation in which I felt totally lost because work at night school had not yet taught me about how the cars operated electrically.

Sovereign Street Permanent Way Yard really felt as if it had not changed since it first opened. Apart from the location being used for official tramcar photographs through the years, the whole place looked fascinatingly old. Whenever I went down there I should not have been surprised to have seen an 'A car' without the 'A' hidden in one of the sheds, i.e. pre-1926, and with it, the platform staff in the uniform of that time, getting the car ready to go on service on Route

No.7-Hyde Park via Belle Vue Road!

Everything in this yard looked old. The buildings, even the people who worked there looked old! The cars that were used as works vehicles were old. They were obviously open-ended cars cut-down to single deck, possibly dating from 1900. What tales they could have told but they always looked so woe-begone that even had they been able to speak to me, I don't think they could have summoned up enough amps to raise a glimmer.

In spite of my discoveries at Torre Road in 1942, I look back to these single-deck works cars and wonder why I never looked INSIDE the cars. Obviously at that time I did not realise the value of historical investigation, therefore I did not examine the cars to try to deduce their origins. I must be thankful that other folk did do thorough research on all the works tramcars.

There were two other vehicles there. I could hardly call them cars, but they were of the type of vehicle that I could climb up on and, had

Plate 95: Sovereign Street Permanent Way Yard, photographed about 1939, but the date could be any time between then and 1948. Note the electric crane, the tippler car minus hoppers, the solid-tyred generator vehicle and the three wheeled Karrier Cob dating from August 1937. The weighbridge at the back of the crane is the location for the photographs of cars 158 (Plate 14) and 272. Leeds City Transport/West Yorkshire Archives Service, Wakefield.

I known about it, be able to feel the history oozing from all the steelwork. These were the remaining tippler cars built at K.D. about 1910. When I found them they looked like trucked underframes with a dash at both ends plus controller and outside brake handle and with two separate side-tipping hoppers, one on each side of the bow-collector tower. I remember standing at the controller of one of them. Rusty, worn and torn.

It is always a shame when a secret is uncovered, leaving nothing to be discovered, but Sovereign Street Yard still felt secret, even to the mobile electric cranes, which, surprisingly, still had trolley booms! The place was a treasure house of a store in my eyes. In there were stacks of new rails, points and crossings, tie-bars, sleepers, overhead line poles and equipment, chains, R.S.J.'s, jim-crows, all manner of steelwork, sand, gravel, stone setts and hidden in the main shed was the capability to fabricate items for a multitude of purposes on the system.

Over the years I had heard that the tippler cars actually rode up a track in Harehills Lane from Roundhay Road to near Salinsky's Factory and then turned left towards what is now Gipton Estate, near Hovingham Allotment Gardens. My father had an allotment on these gardens and certain traces were still visible of adits and tracks. On the way from Milan Road to the garden we walked up Hovingham Avenue on the open side, that is the side facing the waste land past which the track of the tipplers ran. The flagstones on this side of Hovingham Avenue had separated from one another, producing gaps of one inch to one and a half inches between the flagstones. Now, although this had nothing to do directly with the trams the name that was given to these separated flagstones was the 'NIXIPUNKS', current at the same time as my early memories of Leeds cars.

Digressing a bit more from the Drawing Office, another tramway background which I was never able to uncover was that in 1925 to 1928 and 1931 to 1935, Leeds cars were made by Brush at Loughborough and by English Electric at Preston.

The next statement in the description of these cars was that they went into service on such and such a date. How were these double-deck cars, particularly the Middletons, transported to Leeds? How and where were they placed on the tracks in Leeds? Perhaps rather similar to buying a Hornby Train which was lifted out of the box and placed on the railway layout on the table. Where in Leeds was the table and where was the lifting done?

During the preparation in 1993 of an Index for the book by Jim

Plate 96: So this is how it was done! The top and lower decks of Middleton car 261 on separate wagons, leaving the Brush Works at Loughborough in 1934, en route to Leeds. But where in Leeds were the two decks and bogies united? National Tramway Museum Collection.

Soper, Leeds Transport, Volume 1, 1832 - 1902, I read that 'a track connection from Kitson's Works to the Hunslet Road Tramway' was given permission to be laid by the Highways Committee in 1879. Could this be the forerunner of the table?

As I progress through the writing of this story, Hunslet Road seems to have had more than its share of tramway history, some of which was occurring during my lifetime. I was too young to know about all this and my parents would ignore it because Hunslet was on the opposite side of Town and we would have had no reason at all to go anywhere down there. Historical frustration again?

For instance, the cars to Rothwell and Wakefield went along Hunslet Road. That route closed in 1932. We were living in Milan Road at Harehills and could have ridden on the service! The cars to South Accommodation Road reversed before Hunslet Road and returned past the railway yards. This route closed in 1936. We did ride on this route in 1935 (Chapter 1) but my memory of it has almost vanished. When was the track into, say, Kitson's works taken out, because I have no knowledge of it from when I started exploring tram-routes from 1942 onwards.

Before returning to life in the Drawing Office of Tramways in 1943, another digression is worthy of memory. An item on all Leeds

cars which was taken very much for granted by everybody was the
tramcar number as applied to the cars and its style. No other
tramway operator had the same style of figures as Leeds from 1925
(like 400) onwards. The large numbers on the dash at both ends of
the cars and the smaller numbers on the left hand side of the lower
saloon bulkhead (some have been rescued from burning and are at
Crich) and even the smaller numbers on the waist rails of some cars
and on the destination boxes upstairs were all distinctively Leeds,
About 1948, the car numbers on the outside of the cars shrank into
insignificant London Transport-type numbers.... No character!
Cheaper, perhaps, but no character.

As far as I am aware (in 1999) there is only one car left with the
large, characterful, proper Leeds numbers and that is car 345,
presently at Clay Cross in store, waiting for the financial opportunity
to be re-born. I do hope that amongst all the decisions that will take
place about 345 that the proper Leeds numbers can be replaced on
this car.

To return to the thread of this story and to the L.C.T. Drawing
Office and disciplined yesteryear working. My duty every day at
8.31am (one was never late) was to obtain from a particular drawer
the Drawing Index Books and the New Drawings Index Book so that
all the staff could have immediate reference to them. There were two
Drawing Index Books, one for normal size or Main Drawings and the
other for Sketches, i.e. accident plans or bus/tram shelter planning
applications, etc. Sketches were prefixed Sxxxx and the other Main
Drawings from No.1 (in earliest days) to about 55xx when I started
in the Drawing Office.

Drawings of all the Depots were here, including some wonderfully
draughted linens of Swinegate Depot in 1915, drawings of Horsfields
and other cars and many other historical treasures that I would have
liked to linger over but was not allowed to, during working hours.

*Plate 97: The type and style of large numbers on all the cars in the fleet were like
these on balcony car 302 in Swinegate Depot on 19 June 1937.* H.B. Priestley/National
Tramway Museum Collection.

The dinner hour was the time to do that after the top-floor canteen meal.

A considerable number of drawings in early days were on grey tracing cloth and others that had been prepared on faded yellow tracing paper which was so fragile when lying in a horizontal quantity of other drawings on top of the tracing paper. There was no thought then of Vertical Plan Filing, neither was there any thought of standard size drawing sheets. Each drawing was sized according to content.

The filing of all drawings used by everyone in the Drawing Office during the day was the duty of the office juniors at 4.30pm on weekdays and 12noon on Saturdays. We therefore only had thirty minutes to carefully file those precious drawings and woe betide us if ever we got them in the wrong place!

Ronnie and I looked forward to this duty because we could make the filing last almost half an hour - add on tidying the office and washing of dirty hands afterwards.

Tracing paper could be bought fairly easily but we had to be very sparing with the light-blue tracing linen, the most economical use had to be made of this. There was a war on! This light-blue linen came in rolls of about thirty yards and down the edge on both sides of the linen was a red binding thread which had to be removed before the linen could be fixed to the drawing board. Imagine an antiquarian-size piece of linen (the largest listed drawing size at that time) with two pieces of binding thread to be taken off. The thread could be cut off with large scissors or it could be pulled off by hand. If Ronnie or I ever dared to pull it off whilst any of the staff were concentrating on drawing or writing we were verbally 'shot'. The noise this thread made when being released from its linen was almost akin to a present day electric drill going through very hard steel. A sudden rasping noise that upset everybody and if anyone was on the phone, well... ! We learnt something else fast.

The Drawing Indexes were up-dated every Friday afternoon or Saturday morning by Ronnie and myself. Apart from it being a job for juniors, the composition of the Index taught us about the subjects dealt with in the Drawing Office, who drew the plans and why and how they were drawn and with what instruments. We were encouraged to ask questions of the various draughtsmen and to watch them as they used their instruments, pens, etc., to produce lines of even thickness in ink and pencil.

The appropriate new-drawings sheets were removed from the Indexes and along with the rough 'new numbers' Book taken downstairs - two floors - to the typists to be typed up. The General

Manager's Secretary was in charge of the typists. Ronnie and I were suitably polite - or else! The actual walking downstairs to the corridor where the typists were was an adventure in itself because in those early days we were under strict supervision and were not allowed out of the Drawing Office unless specifically instructed apart from going 'down the corridor' as the toilet was known. The toilet door was mahogany too.

The last Drawing Numbers that I remember when I left the Department were in the 7xxx series.

Another duty at 8.31am or even as we went through the door into the Office from the corridor was to switch on the blue-print machine so that the carbon-arc lamp would warm up whilst we attended to the registers, indexes, etc. This meant asking around the other staff if anyone would like a pot (mug) of tea fetching. If the answer was 'yes' - and it invariably was - then a tray was required to carry ten mugs and two pence from each person.

Ronnie or I would then have to go down three floors to the canteen in the basement. We were forbidden to go down in the lift carrying a tray. We were warned not to be seen by any Senior Officer, most certainly not by the General Manager, when we were carrying a trayful of empty, rattling mugs, or worse still, a trayful of full mugs.

If we had ever been seen in the lift with a tray going down past the front door level to the basement and a Senior Officer, Mr J.B. Gill for instance, had to wait until the lift came up again, our fate was almost worse than death! Even worse, if that was possible, Mr Bedell would receive a phone call on the Dictograph from Mr Gill, admonishing him for letting his juniors do such a thing.

We therefore had a double reprimand- Mr Bedell would 'ask' us over to his drawing desk and publicly make sure we understood our misdemeanour and that we also understood that we were not to 'drop me in it again.'

Did I not have an ambition to work 'amongst the trams'? Surely I was working away from the trams. But of course there were compensations, eventually, to this job of mine, once I had mastered the duties that a junior employee was compelled to do.

However, the print machine had warmed up sufficiently by the time we had delivered the tea to everybody. This machine with its horizontal-travelling carbon arc-in-a-glass, had continuous strong fabric belts travelling at right angles to the line of travel of the carbon arc (even this travelled on two rails with four wheels.) The belts extended the full width of the feed and collection tray.

The print paper, only for blue prints, was placed under the tracing

Blue Print Process, called also "ferro-prussiate" or "cyanotype" process. This process, in which salts of iron are used for production of the image, gives a picture of a bright blue colour. One method of preparing it, so that a positive image is obtained from a negative, is as follows:- Good smooth drawing-paper is pinned on to a board and coated by means of a Blanchard brush (q.v.) with:

a.	Potassium ferricyanide	75 grains
	Water	1 oz
b.	Ammonio-citrate of iron	96 grains
	Water	1 oz

Mix equal parts of (a) and (b) for use.

Dry the coated paper in the dark and print under the negative in a printing frame in the ordinary way until the image is clearly seen of a greenish colour. The prints are then well washed in plain water till the high lights are quite white. Rinse in hydrochloric acid 1 dram, water 10 ozs and then again in plain water. The print is then dried. The process, on account of its cheapness and ease of making, is largely used by architects and engineers in copying plans and tracings, etc.

This process was used in the Print Room of the Drawing Office in 1943. (Courtesy Pears Cyclopaedia, 1937 Edition)

to be copied and both were fed into the machine so that the paper would be exposed to the travelling/reversing carbon arc. Correct exposure was only learned through many mistakes. The speed of the arc lamp or of the belts was controlled by two speed-cones near the floor. The belts on these speed-cones had to be manually changed to vary the speed of the belts. After exposure the paper and tracing came out into the curved tray at the front base of the machine. A long, imprecise procedure, the sounds of which remain as fresh in my memory today as the trams themselves.

The exposed print-paper was taken over to the other wall of the print room to a zinc tray which was big enough to take antiquarian-size paper (30" or 40" wide rolls). The print was immersed in a solution in this tray (my memory fails me on what solution) and was uniformly pressed over until the image appeared, white lines on a blue background, when the print was carefully and soggily transferred to a washing tray of clear water (next to the developer tray) and then hung up to dry in a warm cabinet. (See above)

What a process for one print of whatever size, but it was the only process known in those days. It was partly Ronnie's and my job to get to know the machine and how to operate it properly. Eventually a small dyeline machine was obtained and both machines were used

Plate 98: The Chief Traffic Officer of Leeds City Transport, Mr J.B. Gill, left, and Mr A. Stone, Assistant Chief Traffic Officer. Leeds City Transport/West Yorkshire Archives Service, Wakefield.

together. It was most unwise to look directly at the carbon arc for fear of eye damage.

As I have mentioned elsewhere, the period of 45 minutes, twice daily was a basic essential to us of Drawing Office Practice and to our future as proper draughtsmen, no matter what our basic subject, i.e., mechanics or electrics.

The overall instruction to us was that we should each develop (and WILL develop) a STYLE of lettering that would be as distinctive to each person as his fingerprints.

Our draughting apprenticeship would take five years and so it did, albeit with a break of three years after the first sixteen months.

My instructor was Mr Lister of Scholes, a place which I always thought was such a long way away from Leeds. His hand-lettering in ink or pencil was of a very high standard and of a form that appealed to me so I determined to develop my style of lettering in a similar way. What I didn't realise was how long it would take me to learn how to form letters in proportion, in smoothness and at the same time keep the letters vertical and all of the same height.

The engineering-type lettering required in this Drawing Office was always done with a Gillott's size 303 or a Waverley pen nib, using Stephen's black drawing ink. The 303 was a fine nib which produced fine printing in the hands of an experienced draughtsman, but the results of my initial efforts looked as though a one-legged spider had trailed across the tracing cloth. The Waverley nib was a slightly wider nib used for most of our lettering practice. The pen nib was never dipped into the ink bottle. The quill-type squeezable filler was used to apply the correct amount of ink to the pen nib, a very finicky operation which had to be repeated umpteen times during the production of a drawing.

As an addition and as a projection of normal engineering hand-printing, Mr Lister showed me how to form block letters, using the 303 nib, so that I would never need to use artificial aids like stencils or later Letraset.

During the period from September, 1943 to December, 1944 my hand-printing style did not show much development. Verticality and proportion of letters and figures and thus smoothness of appearance on a drawing, did not begin to show itself until I returned to the Drawing Office after three years of military service, when learning how to produce a drawing of good standard which meant good lettering had to be learned all over again. Once learned, however, like learning to ride a bicycle, this hand-printing ability has never left me.

Mr Lister was the Building and Civil Engineering Draughtsman. He was known to some of the older draughtsmen as 'KIPPIS', because it was thought he came from Kippax originally. The rest of the staff in the Drawing Office in late 1943 were -

Mr A.R. Bedell, Chief Draughtsman.
Mr J.R. Blakeborough, Permanent Way Designer plus many other subjects.
Mr D. Kitchen, Artistic Draughtsman, etc.
Mr J. Broadbent, Photographer and General Draughtsman. Known as 'Beeston' because he lived there.
Mr Reginald Theodore Clark, Drawing Office Clerk and general academic, musician and factotum, also called Sam (but not by juniors).
Mr Joe Childs, General Draughtsman.
Mr Brian Marston, Draughtsman. Subject unknown. He left soon after we started.
Mr Ronnie Griffiths, Apprentice Draughtsman, Mechanical Eng^g.
Mr Brian Render, Apprentice Draughtsman, Electrical Eng^g.

Telephone answering was another juniors' duty and our manner-of-answering had to be learnt, as had the voices of callers, especially from within the building. We had to be alert, ready for a message and to be respectful to Senior Officers. We had to learn who were Senior

Officers and who were not and treat them all the same, just in case.

There were three telephones in the office, all in a group on separate small shelves one on each of three sides of one of the two vertical pillars in the office.

One instrument was the National, its name perhaps derived from the National Telephone Company of 1892. This phone was for incoming and outgoing calls from and to the outside world. The instrument was a heavy-based vertical tube about twelve inches high with a vertically-swivelling mouthpiece as part of the instrument. The ear-piece was about five inches long and was hung on a U-shaped hook to the left of the main stem and one leaned forward to speak into the mouthpiece.

A pencil and pad was provided and I have just realised why I always lift a telephone receiver with my left hand. We had to, when using this particular old instrument as we were right handed writers. The bell gave a long-tone ring and the operators were in a room near Reception on the ground floor. No automatic or S.T.D. routines in those days.

The second telephone, the internal, or within the Department, but throughout the system, was a black one with a lift-off type receiver on the top. In place of a dial there was a handle and in order to call the operator, this handle had to be turned clockwise, vigorously, whilst holding the receiver firmly on its rest. This instrument connected the Drawing Office to any of the L.C.T. premises and was the phone we would get through on if, on the odd occasion, we rang in from one of the pole-mounted phone boxes at termini or other locations on the tram routes. The operators were at Crown Point Power Station, near Marsh Lane. The ringing tone sounded as though a spoon was revolving inside a glass dish.

Crown Point was home to the Overhead Lines Foreman and staff, Mr Gabbitas and Mr Bob Burnett, who were supervised by Mr John Burbridge, a very well-known name in Leeds Transport history. Mr Burbridge had an office next to the Drawing Office with a connecting door. His title was Overhead Lines Superintendent. We rarely were involved with this Section.

The third telephone was the Dictograph. We were instructed to pay particular attention to this instrument, which was a brown, rectangular box with the handset on its rest on top of the box. On the vertical front face were ten small, grey levers each about one inch long, all normally horizontal and all having a small rectangular panel under each with a name on it. This was the in-the-building phone. An incoming call buzzed and the receiver was lifted to take the call. To make a call to any of the nine persons out of ten named, the receiver was lifted and the appropriate lever pressed downwards. This automatically buzzed on that person's phone.

The remaining lever was titled very clearly 'General Manager'. It had a white opal bulb below the lever. When the G.M. buzzed this bulb lit up so that there was no doubt who it was at the other end. - Mr W. Vane Morland. This of course was the person whose name I had first seen, long ago on all the trams. Slowly then I was getting nearer to seeing him in person. From my drawing board position I could see this Dictograph and watch what happened when the G.M. buzzed. The instructions to Ronnie and myself were adamant: 'If the light on the Dictograph

Plate 99: The 'National' telephone in the Drawing Office in 1943 was similar to this instrument. Sport and General Press Agency.

shows, the G.M. is calling. Mr Bedell will answer it. If Mr Bedell is not available then Mr Blakeborough will answer it. Both these gentlemen could see the Dictograph from their desks and board positions If neither is about then Mr Lister will RUN the length of the Drawing Office on our shout of 'The Manager!' That buzz had to be answered FAST! The only time Ronnie or I were to answer the G.M.'s buzz was if nobody else was either in or available. We would answer with, 'Drawing Office. Render speaking, Sir!' and tremble in our shoes or stand to attention or both. We had to make sure that we forgot nothing the G.M. said, for he was God. We always wrote down what the G.M. said and placed the note on Mr Bedell's board. My mother had said 'Always write it down' so I always did. As for all being the 'same in the bath'(Chapter 4) these offices had a different bathhouse. We simply did not make calls to the G.M.!

The Chief Traffic Officer at this time, 1943, was Mr J.B. Gill (Plate 98), a small man who made up for lack of physical stature by being a person whom juniors and some seniors did not argue with! The Chief Accountant was Mr C.E. Grayson. We did not come across him much but on the occasional duty we had to carry out for him, he was always courteous to us. Our departmental Head was Mr T. Ellis, the Constructional Engineer. Mr Ellis was always correct in appearance and manner and was always a gentleman. We were in constant contact for all manner of duties which we carried out for him as quickly and correctly as possible. Mr H.P. Foster was his predecessor. Mr T.H. Parkinson was Rolling Stock Engineer, Buses and was based at Donisthorpe Street Bus Works. Only occasionally would he come into the Drawing Office. Mr J. Burbridge was the Overhead Line Superintendent and was responsible to Mr Ellis. Mr Burbridge's instructions were carried out correctly and quickly too! All these gentlemen (Senior Officers) were addressed as 'Sir', at least until I came back from the Forces.

To make sure we knew how to answer this Dictograph and for us to understand what happened at both ends of a call, we were taken by Mr Lister to another Senior Officer's room when it was known that the gentleman was out (and would be for a while). Here we would practice making and receiving calls from the Drawing Office, one of us at either end of the phone, but making sure that the incoming buzz at either end was one of us and not someone else coincidentally ringing the Senior Officer or the Drawing Office. We were learning, fast!

I remember that shortly after this, to complete our telephone education, so to speak, we were allowed, and accompanied, down to the G.M.'s Secretary, Mildred who had been asked by Mr Lister to let us see and hear how a call was made to the Drawing Office from the G.M.'s office, one day when the great man was away. Mr Bedell knew about this, of course.

This visit was a first-class experience for two juniors, as may be imagined. We would never, normally have been allowed anywhere along the G.M.'s corridor unless we had committed some heinous crime.

The G.M.'s room was mahogany. He had a very large photograph of 255 on one wall. It took me thirty-five years before I had a photograph of 255 on my wall at home and that was by courtesy of Nottingham University Photographic Unit.

However, we were shown what to do with the Dictograph which did not have a white light on any lever. Ronnie and I pretended that we were the 'G.M. here' for a few exciting minutes. The ways of this Drawing Office were sometimes unorthodox, but we never forgot what we were shown or what we learned there. The telephone instruments were cleaned once a week by a brown-overalled girl from the firm PHONOTAS, which was established in 1911 by George Leslie Becker.

On 19 February 1994, some of the furniture and fittings from the G.M.'s office were retrieved by Leeds Transport Historical Society and is now safely kept at the National Tramway Museum at Crich. Well done. I'm sure Mr W Vane Morland would have approved! The comparisons between 1943 and 1993 in attitudes to work, discipline and technicalities are unbelievable. I am sure, in hindsight, that the strict discipline in the Drawing Office stood me in good stead for that period of my life which I knew had to come in about a year's time. I had to put thoughts of call-up out of my mind and get on with learning about Leeds City Transport. I had no idea about what part of the Forces I would be going into. There was no choice, I was told.

Fairly soon after starting work at L.C.T. in September 1943 I had worked out the best and the most interesting ways of travelling to work in Head Office to arrive before 8.30am. There were three tram routes I could use, all three using a different type. of tramcar. One way was to walk down Karnac Road, turn left down the unmade Nice View to the Sorting Office in Harehills Road and get on a car there at 7.55am. The car would be going to 9-Dewsbury Road via Corn Exchange and could have been a Pivotal, a balcony car, a Hull car, an un-air-braked convert or even, though unlikely 276 or 389. The journey could be fraught with delay, due to the single track and loops in Beckett Street. Whatever interesting car I was on or what

Plate 100: The Chief Accountant of Leeds City Transport, Mr C.E. Grayson, right, and Mr A.S. Binns, Assistant Chief Accountant. Leeds City Transport/West Yorkshire Archives Service, Wakefield.

cars may have been seen en route or even what out-of-the-ordinary happenings may have occurred on the journey to town, delay was unthinkable for me because we were not allowed to be late into Head Office. The signing-in machine would prove lateness as if walking fast into the Drawing Office would not be noticed by Mr Bedell.

An excuse or reason that the 9-Dewsbury Road car was delayed in Beckett Street was never accepted: 'You must always allow for delays and set off earlier or use another route.'

So, having gone through that admonishment once, I resolved never to be caught napping again.

The second way to get to work was to walk right down Karnac Road to Harehills Corner and get on any car that came from Clock Buildings, that is cars from Easterly Road or Roundhay, and which were going down Briggate, i.e. a 1-Lawnswood or a 4-Hawksworth Road (or short workings thereof) all going via Sheepscar and North Street to Briggate Barriers where I got off and walked, or ran, across Boar Lane/Briggate Junction down Lower Briggate to Head Office.

I was never late using these routes but at 7.55am, all the cars going down to Town were nearly full before I got on them, even those only coming from Easterly Road. Most likely I would have to sit on an aisle seat upstairs and see nothing of other cars on the run to town or strap-hang inside and try and look-out-front through the sliding door to the driver's platform. Not a very good way to go to work - squashed in with, say, seventy other persons. One reason why all these cars were full was because the business area of Leeds was west of Briggate. Not many folk from Roundhay or Oakwood worked east of Briggate at that time In any case no cars ran from Roundhay or Oakwood to Vicar Lane, etc., east of Briggate.

So all this was a deterrent to my using these routes as I always wanted to get a seat at either the front or back upstairs in order to see as many other cars and happenings on the way to Town. The third way proved the best. I decided to set off from home even earlier and walk down Harehills Lane to Roundhay Road, turn right and go to the Easterly Road terminus of the cars from Beeston. Cars from Kirkstall turned here too but the 5-Beeston car was my objective.

For reasons best known to the scheduling staff at Swinegate Depot, the car that was due to leave Easterly Road at about 7.55am on 5-Beeston was always a P.22, that is a Leeds-built car of 1923/1925. This duty never varied and by getting on the car at the start of the journey I almost always got a front seat upstairs next to and left of the destination box. Blast netting notwithstanding, to see-out-front was still important and the seat above the stairs was identical with that on 399 at Crich today. If any of the six cars with reversed stairs turned up then the front seat on the right-hand side of the destination box had to suffice. (Cars 370 to 375).

Another factor that influenced my use of this route was that in spite of the time of day being the start of the rush-hour, this Beeston car was never overloaded because the car went down Vicar Lane to Corn Exchange. Mostly I got off at the Corn Exchange in order to walk along Duncan Street to Boar Lane/Briggate Junction to take in the cars on all the routes that interchanged at this busy place. A short walk or run down Lower Briggate made sure I was never late signing in.

This Beeston car was very rarely late getting to town and I was able to take note of all the cars seen en-route, to check my Book, without looking at my watch all the time.

Gradually I became familiar with and quite attached to these P.22s. There was a different car at Easterly Road most mornings and it was very interesting to note each car's details, I didn't think about paint-dates until I had all their information written into the Book.

399, one of those P22s, is at the National Tramway Museum at Crich, Derbyshire and I am glad to say that it has been beautifully and expensively restored. It is not at all difficult, fifty years later, to imagine myself back on 399 plus anti-blast netting in Leeds at 8.00am, intentionally going to Corn Exchange. Now, back to the Drawing Office again.

In a room off the mahogany corridor leading to the Drawing Office and adjacent to the fire-escape was the Photographic Dark Room, which was the retreat of Mr Broadbent. On the odd occasions when I was allowed in this Dark Room I saw hundreds of glass-plate negatives in boxes. Pure wishful thinking but I had to restrain my curiosity and tramway-interest instincts to remove the lot and have them copied. It would have been impossible, of course. There was no likelihood of the trams in Leeds being scrapped, was there? So all these negatives would be perfectly safe? Well! Where are these negatives now? Destroyed? On the same theme, where are all the drawings that Ronnie Griffiths and myself so carefully prepared, recorded and filed between 1943 and 1950?

All staff at Head Office had to sign-in on a clock machine, one for each floor, when coming in up to 8.30am. We had to sign-out and in at the dinner-hour and out when going home at 5.00pm. Any overtime was also signed in and out.

The period from September 1943 to March 1944 was a probationary period for me and a learning period. I knew my job was temporary and that only by being successful as a learning junior would I be allowed to return to the Drawing Office of L.C.T. after service in the Forces, however long that would be. Nothing was really certain. It was wartime and anything could happen to change one's direction of ambition. So this period was one of hard work as Mr Ellis had said it would be, constantly aware of the obligation to carry out every duty, however small or however important, to the best of our ability. When a mistake was made, and there were many, our name was mud. Too many muddy-names and we would be taken in front of Mr Ellis. We were marched in and stood straight, ready for a right going-over. We came out, having had a going-over and walked back along the mahogany corridor feeling about six inches tall, resolving never to land ourselves in that situation again.

The world outside L.C.T. Head Office, my tramcar world, had to take second place but at night, never mind the blackout, and at weekends there was time to explore Leeds and ride on tram routes, like 19-Lower Wortley, that I did not know. We were issued with travel tokens when we went out on a job during office hours on either the trams or buses and sometimes one or two of these would be left over. This would allow me to make a trip, say, to Beeston from Harehills to explore the route without homework worries for the next day and to enjoy the car concerned. The car on this route could have been a P35, or a P.22 or a Convert or even 275 or 321.

Now that I worked for the 'Department', it made all the difference to me during these rides of exploration when not on duty. It was a most pleasant feeling of belonging, what I had always wanted to do from knowing about 255, ten years ago.

On these rides on strange routes whenever possible I sat upstairs at the front so that I could see as much as possible and yet be aware of what the driver was doing in his handling of the car and how he reacted to the sparse traffic conditions. Although I had driven cars to Elland Road and was aware of the principles of driving the cars, nobody in Head Office was aware of that. It was my secret and it remained so, as far as I knew. By watching the driver on my car, it was possible to learn more and more in readiness for the next opportunity I would have to drive a Leeds tramcar.

Chapter Nine

WORKING FOR THE TRAMS

In the streets of Leeds that had tram tracks laid in them an accepted hazard over the years was the appearance from time to time of grey/white barriers with the words 'Road Guard' on the top bar. These barriers were suitably placed at protective intervals round a long hole in the roadway in which was exposed tram rails, points and crossings of a tram junction.

'Oh! they're repairing the tram tracks again', would be the comment. Apart from seeing these repairs in various places, any thoughts I had about the rails were only fleeting. The tracks were taken for granted like the cars that ran on them. They were there in the roadway, we walked over them, sometimes we got our cycle wheels trapped in the grooves, the trams ran on them and we tried to put pennies on the flat rail for the cars to flatten them. The tram tracks had been there for years and, no doubt, always would be. They were part of city life. So when the Permanent Way Engineer said that we were to assist him on a track survey at a particular junction we had no idea what he meant, nor could we possibly imagine what was

Plate 101: Car 245 at the junction of Bishopgate Street and Neville Street with Swinegate en route into service from Swinegate Depot in 1948. This junction was the site of a track survey on an exceptionally cold Sunday morning in 1949. R.F. Mack.

involved! The engineer then explained that when a trackwork junction was showing signs of wear and tear it would not be very long before the existing trackwork would have to be taken out and new trackwork put in. In ample time before the estimated time of replacement a survey of the junction was required, the survey then being drawn out in the Drawing Office from the site measurements. Then, to fit the existing tracks on each of the roads leading to the junction, a new design of trackwork was necessary. In some locations the new design had also to fit in with a new alignment of kerbs and other road improvements, particularly after the war.

Ronnie and I were told that surveys that were carried out at some junctions were done by L.C.T. staff. At complicated junctions like City Square and Boar Lane / Briggate, the surveys would be done by engineers from the trackwork manufacturers of Sheffield. In some cases new trackwork was built-up in Sovereign Street Permanent Way yard for small junctions or curves like Harper Street or, at a later date, St. Chad's Road, Headingley. All this instruction was leading to our initiation into this new and very exciting subject of trackwork surveying, installation and maintenance. Now, in 1999, it may be that there is no one else around who took part in these surveys, so, for the

Map 5: Shows the overall location of the track survey of 26 October 1947. By kind permission of the Ordnance Survey, Southampton.

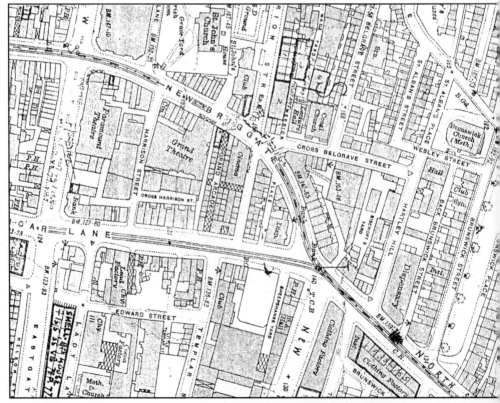

Plate 102: City Square in wartime emptiness. Note the white kerb edges and pole bases, white fender on car 176 and car 6 in khaki in late 1942. Yorkshire Post.

record, this important part of tramway operation is described here fully, before another hidden necessity of Leeds Tramways is lost forever. In 1943/1944 when we first learned about this unknown aspect of Tramways, I thought that at last I would be involved in a very practical way actually doing something for the benefit of the trams or working for the trams that I had called my trams. No matter how many surveys I was ultimately involved in, I always felt the same way about them.

The Permanent Way Engineer supervised the surveys done by Leeds Tramways. Mr Machin was the surveyor for Edgar Allen's and Mr Masterman was Hadfield's surveyor. In each case Ronnie and I were assistants, dogsbodies or flagwaggers, learning very fast, in spite of this totally new exercise, so as not to waste the surveyor's time, or in some locations, so as not to create any more hazards than there were already. The most detailed and time-consuming survey in which we were involved was Boar Lane / Briggate Junction. The comparison between this location and City Square was not in complexity but in site compression. City Square was spacious whereas Boar Lane / Briggate was confined within a right-angled cross-roads with fixed, close kerb and building lines. The survey here, possibly taking eight hours, involved two Permanent Way safety men and flags, with our engineer and ourselves working to the instructions of either Mr Machin or Mr Masterman.

Either of these gentlemen would come over to Leeds, stay

overnight and meet us on site on the Sunday morning. Sheffield, in those days of ordinary roads and proper train services was a different world away from Leeds - 35 miles was a long way then. Both gentlemen had different overall methods of surveying but they both had one important thing in common. They were both infinitely patient and precise in their routine. They had to be, of course, because there could on no account be any variation in gauge on new trackwork. Such variation that did occur afterwards was caused by poor trucks, wear by wheel flanges and, most difficult of all to correct, bad driving and thoughtless braking.

When working with the Sheffield surveyors we learned to be just as precise and thorough, thus gaining experience that we continued to apply on future surveys. This particular aspect of tramway work was most satisfying, quite exhilarating, sometimes entertaining and many times with exposure to risk from moving traffic. This latter item may explain why, in later years, I so much enjoyed point-duty control of traffic at busy intersections at the end of football matches, cricket matches and other public events or displays, etc. Very few of the trackwork surveys seemed to be done in good weather. Most were in the autumn but the rain, wind and cold which, combined with traffic hazards, made us dusty, or splashed, or both, were nothing compared to standing, crouching or kneeling in the middle of the roads and tracks and knowing that I was working for the trams' benefit.

This was a side of Tramways that few people knew existed. Before joining Tramways I certainly did not. This work became more worthwhile, almost secret. It certainly felt secret starting work on site at 7 o'clock on a Sunday morning when there was hardly anyone about and if we dropped a steel tape on the roadway the noise echoed between the buildings.

An example of a track survey by L.C.T. staff is the one we carried out at the junction of North Street / Vicar Lane / New Briggate / New York Road on Sunday, October 26th, 1947, when I was on leave from my Regiment - we were keen in those days! We had done a few surveys before this, but my diary entry for this day confirms the date and location. (See Plate 104)

The area around the tracks on the four roadways was spacious. Along North Street cars on routes 1, 4 , 5 and 8 came towards the junction. Routes 1 and 4 turned up New Briggate. Routes 5 and 8 went down Vicar Lane. Down New Briggate, cars on routes 2, 2 circular, 3 and 3 circular came towards the junction, whilst up Vicar Lane, cars on routes 3 and 6 came to the junction. There were no tracks in New York Road, but up here came bus routes from outside

Leeds. The buses did not cross any tram tracks but they did need to swing out and wide to clear the acute-angled corner from New York Road into Vicar Lane. A preliminary visit to this junction showed that from 7.00am to 9.00am on a Sunday, services on routes 1, 2c, 3, 3c and 4 were not very frequent and were even less frequent on routes 5, 6 or 8. From 9.00am onwards the frequency on all these routes gradually increased so that there was hardly more than five minutes between cars passing over the junction in one direction or another, at a time when our measuring tapes would be fully extended. There were, of course, a number of other road vehicles passing over the junction, but generally this traffic would not be excessive.

The tracks in North Street towards the junction were fairly straight on a slight slope up. The tracks in New Briggate were on a sharper slope down and also curved left to the junction and on to North Street. The tracks in Vicar Lane came uphill gently right to the junction. The junction was controlled by robots (traffic lights) and the incoming points were driver-controlled. There were a considerable number of overhead line poles on the kerb-edges here and numerous inspection covers and manhole covers for various public utilities in the roadways. There were also at least two, if not three section points on the overhead line. The scene was thus set in our minds and we could begin to think about the equipment we should need and the time we should start on site in order to complete the survey before the traffic of all kinds made our working in the roadways more difficult.

A survey at a junction like this could take about 6 or 7 hours, dependent on site conditions and on whether the junction was to be replaced as it was now or whether any re-alignment or alterations were to be made to the track layout which could require a greater amount of roadway, footpath and manhole details to be measured up. The positions of any other street furniture that would be affected would need to be noted. The positions of existing overhead line poles had to be located as any re-alignment of track may well cause the overhead to be repositioned too.

There obviously was a great deal of thinking ahead to be done in planning the method of survey and also in preparing the equipment we would need. We put it all together in the Drawing Office beforehand so that early on the Sunday morning all we had to do was to pick it up and travel, preferably on the front platform of a service car, to site.

The day before, i.e. on the Saturday morning working at Head Office, Ronnie and I gathered together the items required and laid them out on the floor of the Drawing Office, according to the Kit List which experience had shown was needed to avoid mistakes or forgetfulness. We could not afford to forget anything, not for fear of wrath decending on us - it would! But because of the nuisance and waste of time of having to RUN back to Head Office from the survey site for the missing item. If we were working in the centre-ish of Leeds, this run-back could only take a few minutes. If we were further away then our name was MUD! It was a bit muddy anyway in the fashion of juniors of the day (irrespective of military service!).

The kit-list was: theodolite and tripod, 2 x 100'-0" steel tapes, one 100'-0" linen tape, string line, field book, lumps of soft-chalk, hard-chalk sticks, pencils (one for sighting from the theodolite and therefore with a long sharp point and not to be used for anything else). Further pencils, pencil sharpener, penknife, soft rubber, hammer, a sharp cold-chisel, cloths, red flags and aluminum tripod flag supports, other survey books and pads.

For ourselves, gloves with no finger-ends, heavy shoes or boots, jerseys and raincoats with sou-westers. There was no 'Goretex' invented then and high-visibility vests were unheard of. No safety regulations, we just used our common sense, our sense of anticipation (psychic) and of preservation. Flasks of tea and some buns completed the items.

In the Drawing Office we set up the theodolite on its tripod with plumb-bob and checked that all the knurled brass knobs were clean and operating correctly, i.e. no threads damaged, and that the lenses were clean. Then the engineer checked it over and at the same time checked the rest of the equipment bearing in mind the survey location. We unwound the string-line to check for any signs of fraying or wear.

One of us would be detailed to go down to Sovereign Street Permanent Way Yard for more rags or cloths and for lumps of soft-chalk. If I was the lucky one for this walk I used it to look quickly round the Yard to keep tabs on vehicles, etc. I returned to the Drawing Office by walking through the entire length of Swinegate Depot, especially if it was raining so as to keep the chalk and cloths dry. At least, that was the stated reason but for me it was the excuse to see what cars were in the Depot and that included 'strangers'.

The Permanent Way Foreman, whose office was in the Yard, was a dour person, always dressed in dark trousers and a black Crombie-like top coat and a greyish trilby. I do not remember seeing him either smile or walk fast!

Back then to the Drawing Office to put the theodolite away in its purpose-made wooden case and leather carrying strap for shoulders. The string-line was re-wound on to its 10-inch-long piece of brush-handle-type wood with rounded ends and a nick in one end (like a cotton bobbin), to secure the loose string-end. Everything was put ready to pick up at 6.30am on the Sunday morning. The Permanent Way Engineer, Ronnie and myself were thus committed to getting up at 5.15am on the Sunday (next day). This was another part of our training, disciplining oneself to be up on time, in spite of being at the Kingsway or Clock Cinemas on the Saturday night. On the Sunday morning my mother always produced a three-course breakfast because she said that if I was: 'Full, warm and dry, I would not harm!'

That statement has been proven so many times when walking on Scottish or Welsh mountains or when, preferably, walking on the North Pennine Fells of North Yorkshire. My mother and father were just as interested in my activities in Tramways and gave me much encouragement and stickability.

Once full and warm my cycle ride to Town was down to Roundhay Road to Roseville Road, past the West Yorkshire bus garage to Sheepscar Street South, up to North Street and down Vicar Lane instead of uphill to New Briggate top. There were robots to delay my

Plate 103: The tram track junction of New Briggate (left), North Street (ahead) and Vicar Lane (right) in 1939. On the day of our track survey in 1947 very little had changed here. H.B. Priestley/National Tramway Museum Collection.

progress down Briggate even at 6.30am on a quiet morning like a Sunday. Then down Call Lane to Swinegate Depot to put my bike in the racks near Mr Pegram's box. The very fact of riding down to Town at that time of day was exciting, empty, echoing and silent. A city-bound tramcar setting off from Benson Street near Golden Cross to come up North Street could be heard quite clearly at the Dispensary. The car type was recognisable too - by its sound.

Mr Pegram's board that showed which cars were on which tracks sometimes showed a 'strange' car. I'd be quick and have a look at the car. For instance the P.35 - 165 never came off 14-Stanningley, but if I saw it on the board I'd ask questions. Perhaps it was en route to Kirkstall Works.

All this curiosity could only take five minutes as I had to be upstairs in the Drawing Office, after signing-in, of course, in order to bring down the equipment in the lift. At that time of day I was allowed to operate the lift, too, so long as nobody of influence saw me.

Then, perhaps, we would be taken to site in one of the Permanent Way vehicles - a lorry or a smaller vehicle arranged by the Engineer. Preferably though I would run across again to Swinegate Depot and find out if any cars were going on first duty on 6-Meanwood. If so, then with permission of the driver (even better if we knew the driver) we put all the equipment on the front end of the car and then sat downstairs (inside) so that we could see-out-front (as in 1933 onwards).

If the driver was kind and most of them were, some knew Ronnie's father, he would stop for us to unload the equipment actually at the junction and not at the Dispensary stop, over a hundred-yards-of-carrying-equipment away. At the end of the survey we did not sit inside a car, we were too dirty! Employees of L.C.T. had to set a good example. So some other way of returning to Swinegate was devised. Sometimes we were able to stand on the driver's platform! Even if I felt tired or wet or just dirty, the opportunity to stand on the front platform magically got rid of any weariness. Here was excitement again!

When the equipment was off-loaded and placed safely, we stood at the junction, in the middle of the tracks to assess the feel of the location and to decide where the main survey lines should go. Some locations felt difficult, some were distinctly hostile, some were in order. These impressions were not caused by people, but rather by an atmosphere due to the type of district. This junction was open and very much in order. It was obvious, however, that as the morning progressed, so would the number of cars in service increase and therefore we anticipated problems at the times we would have the steel tape at full length. We had to have eyes in the back of our heads at this place.

So we got cracking by running out the string-line from its tying-point round an overhead line pole, so that one of us could 'chalk-the-line' ready for 'plinking'. The engineer placed the theodolite and plumb-bob at a point on the junction where a survey-line, set out from New Briggate, would cross the survey-lines set out from North Street and Vicar Lane. This position was between the tracks towards North Street but as near as possible to the middle diamond of the crossing.

In almost all double-track junction surveys this was a most vulnerable position for the instrument because trams would be passing very close in both directions. At this site there was a greater distance between the tracks from the junction towards the Dispensary than the normal four feet. The legs of the theodolite tripod were in less danger of being hit by any loose part of a tram's lifeguard, etc. and also less likely to be affected by any vibration through the ground as a car thumped over the crossing or points. Fortunately there was not much other traffic and what there was tended to steer to the left-hand side of tram-rails, especially when they were worn or could be seen to be raised slightly above the road surface, due to wear and tear. There were very few folk about, we were not keen on 'gawpers'.

Next, one of us walked along North Street in the four foot (although here it was between five and six feet) to find a suitable point within the length of the string-line to place a sharp-pointed pencil vertically on the road surface which the engineer could sight on to. If that pencil-point position was considered suitable the other one of us chiselled a cross in the road surface at that pencil-point. This cross was chalked (A).

The same was done up New Briggate, where the chiselled cross was marked (B) and again down Vicar Lane. The chiselled cross here was marked (C). The point of the instrument's plumb-bob was also chiselled and marked as intersection (X). Thus we had four points marked on the road that could not be obliterated by rain or rubber tyres. The angles between all three lines were accurately measured and recorded by the engineer.

From the back of the instrument, the string-line, heavily-chalked, was run out under the instrument to point A in North Street, with Ronnie at one end of the line and myself at the other. The string-line

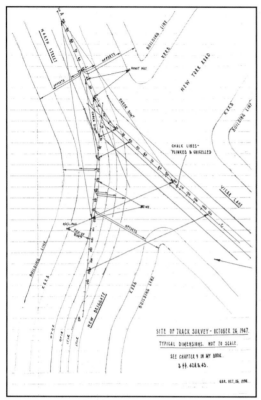

Plate 104: A drawing based upon our track survey at North Street, New Briggate and Vicar Lane in 1947. This is not to scale but may give an idea of the setting out and dimensions necessary for this type of survey. Author.

was placed under one's instep which allowed us to swivel the line by twisting our foot to right or left in order to position the line, first, over the cross X. When that was correct, the person's foot at the other end of the string-line was suitably swivelled to align the string on the cross A, all the time keeping the string-line taut and just off the ground. Once the line was over both crosses it was pulled as taut as possible and the engineer went to about half-way between intersection X and point A. He lifted the string-line against our pulling it taut and let it snap down on the road surface. This we called 'plinking the line'. The resultant chalk line on the road gave us our first survey line, in this case down North Street. Throughout this five-minute procedure we could not move out of the way of any vehicle, so we hoped the tram drivers would be patient. Most of them were, but just occasionally one driver, who would not know that he and we were on the same firm, was 'bolshy'. Of course he then came up against the Permanent Way Engineer and found himself waiting longer and possibly later on, being asked to have a 'conversation' with Mr J.B. Gill, the Chief Traffic Officer! Not a pleasant experience for an impatient driver!

If the atmosphere was damp or there was any inclination to rain, the string-line was then wound in quickly and covered up and the 100 foot steel tape, which was well-oiled, was used to measure out from intersection X every 10 feet to about 120 feet along survey-line A. Each of these 10 foot points was chiselled in the roadway, and numbered A10, A20, A30 etc. We now had a fixed line that any rain could not obliterate. All dimensions were in feet and inches, no metric rubbish in those days!

The same procedure was carried out for survey lines B and C, New Briggate and Vicar Lane, respectively. During this time it was noticed that, gradually, more trams were coming into service and one or two other vehicles were appearing on our bit of road. That was all very well until they tried to drive over either the string-line or, even worse, the steel tape. The string-line, if run over only made false chalk marks on the road when passed over by rubber tyres. The steel tape did not snap if rubber tyres went over it when it was flat on the ground, but if front rubber tyres went over the tape fast they would cause the tape to whip on to its side and the back rubber tyres would snap the tape. Then the air was blue because the driver of the offending vehicle was suddenly found to be blind and to have no parents! The tape was now useless. It was discarded and the spare 100-foot tape rapidly came into use. Needless to say if a tramcar went over the string-line, steel tape or linen tape (when occasionally used), each snapped at once under the steel wheels. Of course it was entirely up to us to make sure by keeping a sharp lookout that no vehicle crossed the line. We became street-wise very quickly. Whether the atmosphere was wet or dry, it was good policy to chisel the lines as quickly as possible. The chiselling was a safety precaution in another way too, because when drawing out the survey later, if any dimensions were suspect, we could always go back to that particular point without having to set the survey up again (perish the thought). I do not ever remember having to check anything again. If that had been necessary if would have had to have been on the Tuesday morning following the Sunday survey (Monday was drawing-out day). Traffic would have been busier, certainly there would have been more trams and so we would have needed a flag-wagger with red flag to cover us. He would be from the Permanent Way gang from Sovereign Street Yard, most likely 'borrowed' from another job which would not have pleased the Permanent Way Foreman. Our names would have been MUD again!

Continuing the survey, from each 10 foot point on the first survey-line A down North Street, i.e. from A10, A20, A30 etc, we took dimensions called offsets, at right-angles to the survey line to the kerb-edge and the back of the footpath on one side of North Street, i.e. the shortest dimension. To determine exactly where that was, we were commanded by the engineer to 'swing it' - nothing whatever to do with Glenn Miller!

We did the same swings to the outgoing (from Town) track, outside rail (OTOR), then to the outgoing track, inside rail (OTIR), all from the survey-line A. The dimensions were taken to the nearest 1/32" to the gauge line, allowing for rail wear.

This longest-dimension-first, relative to the survey-line was part of the discipline of operating a steel tape. Nothing was allowed to drive or even walk over the tape, but discretion was used if any service cars approached whilst the tape was laid across the tracks. It was invariably wise to let the car go - they did have a schedule to keep to.

The foregoing dimensions from the point of intersection X were similarly taken from the furthest 10 foot point on survey-line A along North Street back towards the intersection, that is from A120 to A10 and X, along the incoming track (to Town), outside rail (ITOR) and then to the incoming track, inside rail (ITIR). The dimensions were swung to the kerb edge and the back of the footpath on this side of the road too. That then completed the main dimensions along North Street.

The same routine was followed up New Briggate and down again to the intersection X on survey-line B. Also the similar method on survey-line C down Vicar Lane and back again to intersection X. This last set of dimensions were the longest in individual length as Vicar Lane was wider here than any other section of this survey. It was in this part that the out-of-Town buses swung out and round from New York Road, so we had to be particularly careful when we heard the bus engines as they came up New York Road to the robots. The buses were double-deck, West Yorkshire Road Car Company and had Bristol engines which were easily identifiable by their particular engine note. We therefore had plenty of 'audible warning of approach!' of the buses on their last few yards towards their Bus Station further down Vicar Lane.

So we had to have eyes in the back of our heads as we bent down in the road concentrating on reading or holding the tape correctly. The robots at the road junction helped us to get some of the longer dimensions read.

Another pleasant 'hazard' was the fact that the junction was not far away from Thorne's Toffee Factory at the back of New York Road and from time to time we could smell and almost taste the toffee. Having completed the longest part of the survey, there was time for tea and buns, having put the theodolite in a safe place and where we could summarise the operation so far and plan the next stages.

Next then were the check dimensions between survey-lines. These were fairly long tape-lengths and demanded very watchful eyes on all traffic. They were taken from survey-line A point A20, to point B20 on survey-line B, and from point B20 to point C20 on survey-line C.

Back again from point C20 to point A20 thus triangulating the survey-lines for the first time. The second time the dimensions were taken from point A40 to B40, B40 to C40 and C40 back to A40.

We always tried for a third set of check dimensions, assuming no obstacles to the 'run' of the tape, on any survey, but in this situation, 60 feet from the intersection point X, up Briggate was too far up to allow the tape a straight 'run' to C60 in Vicar Lane. Various walls, or railings or other fixed objects were in the way. The dimension A60 to C60 was longer than the steel tape and the dimension itself was right across the top of New York Road. It was too risky and also too inaccurate as the tape would have had to have been laid twice and in view of the situation, two lengths of the tape would not necessarily have produced an absolutely straight line at the 100 foot temporary mark. There could also have been a very small gap, unidentified, between the end of one tape run and the second. The dimension was not taken. There were three other checks we had taken accurately, they were deemed sufficient.

In further sequence, the next series of dimensions were to locate drain boxes, manholes or other inspection covers which were in the roadway. This was done in each case by taking dimensions from two of the points on the appropriate survey-line to both nearest corners of a square or rectangular box (and measure the box) or to the centre of a circular box, plus the diameter thereof. The positions of overhead line poles, telegraph poles and section boxes for the overhead section points and point controls were located in the same way, as were the robots (traffic lights) positions.

Finally the toes of the track points in North Street were located, again from two points on survey-line A. The track points were almost in line with the robot pillars on the footpath at Hirsch's building on the corner of North Street and New York Road.

Amongst all this concentration on the survey itself, there were moments which broke the severity of the situation. An example was when we were measuring out the 10 foot points on the string-line chalk mark of survey-line B in, or up, New Briggate.

Ronnie was holding one end of the tape on the intersection point X and I was holding the other (100 foot) end of the tape that distance away up the slope of New Briggate. We were both pulling the tape tight and at the same time looking out to make sure that no vehicles ran over the tape. Once having got the tape tight on the 'plinked' string-line, the engineer went along the string-line, marking each 10 foot position with a sharpened piece of hard chalk - all part of the survey routine, of course. I was crouching on my haunches, facing down New Briggate with both hands on the road surface holding the steel tape flat. Our engineer was facing at right-angles to the line of tape and road. Only Ronnie was able to see what was behind me. Now, we had got to know various drivers quite well through our jobs outside and also because Ronnie's father was a driver. When one or two of the drivers realised who we were and when they came across us in the physical positions as I have described above, they threw-off as they came up and over New Briggate top towards North Street and coasted, on the hand-brake, slowly and silently right up to a yard from my back. (Can you imagine a 12 ton tramcar coasting SILENTLY? If gravity assists, I assure you they can do just that!)

Often I could sense a car was behind me, but I couldn't move because the tape was being held tight and flat on the ground. Our engineer wouldn't see the car, he was concentrating on marking the 10 foot points accurately. Ronnie saw the car and he would realise what was afoot from previous episodes, so held on tight to his end of the tape and waited for the inevitable to happen.

The driver of the car behind me knew that I couldn't move so, suddenly, he stamped on the gong!! Well, I jumped in spite of myself and the tape flew all over, even though I had the tape case held firmly. Realising then who the driver was, we all had a good laugh, especially Ronnie who could see what was coming. All, that is except our engineer. The drivers did this as a bit of fun, but also to upset our engineer which a thing like this always did. The traffic staff knew him well.

Once the survey was complete to the engineer's satisfaction, the steel-tape was cloth-cleaned by the side of the road, the string-line rubbed lightly so that chalk-dust would fly about outside, rather than back in the Drawing Office. The theodolite was wiped over, dismantled and packed up, plus plumb-bob and all equipment made ready to go back to Swinegate Head Office.

One final observation. Eventually on these surveys it was a source of pride to Ronnie and myself that we knew what was happening so well that we could anticipate one another's moves and we could therefore be continuous in measuring, without being told and without wasting time and causing the engineer to erase things in his field book. He would be quite niggly (with justification) if we did cause this to happen. One negative thing, we were never allowed to read the theodolite!

A phone call from one of the pole-mounted L.C.T. phone boxes to Sovereign Street to arrange, if possible, a vehicle to collect us would have been the best, but I tried always to persuade our engineer that we should carry the equipment over to the tram stop at the Ritz Cinema in Vicar Lane and wait for a car on route 5-Beeston or route 8-Elland Road. We could put the equipment on the front of the car and ride on the front platform (especially if the car was a Beeston Convert and had 'doors-on') actually down to Lower Briggate / Swinegate Junction. This was much more exciting - it was another opportunity to ride on the normally-forbidden driver's platform. From Swinegate junction it wasn't far then to carry all the equipment into Head Office. We had, of course, unloaded the equipment from the front of the car and that was almost in the middle of the Swinegate Junction. Imagine that nowadays!

Once back in the Drawing Office, possibly at 2.00pm on a Sunday afternoon, one of us would dash downstairs to the canteen for three huge mugs of tea and come up in the lift: there were no Senior Officers about on a Sunday. Thus warmed up we cleaned the steel tape and re-greased it. We cleaned the instrument thoroughly before going home, after signing out, of course. Thus ended another of those exciting events which occurred every so often during my working for the trams. Always exciting, sometimes unorthodox, but a necessary part of the tramway world, a world I had looked forward to becoming part of for such a long time.

A junction like North Street/New Briggate/Vicar Lane or the one at Armley Road/Wellington Road or those similar double-track junctions elsewhere in the City were all fairly straightforward surveys but their locations made things different, sometimes even tiresome, but the work was enjoyable, frozen fingers or not. The extent of any survey and the weather were always a challenge to us, but if the drawing-out of the survey was to be done in our Drawing Office, we watched it and were very chuffed when dimensions fitted in, - the rain and cold forgotten already.

Strangely, we were never told and, again, I never thought to ask about how and where the manufacture of the replacement trackwork for any of the ordinary junctions was carried out. We were told when the work on site was scheduled and we were encouraged to be there overnight on the weekend when the new junction was laid-in. (I didn't need any encouragement to be out all night on the tracks!) I always thought trackwork at 'O' gauge or 'OO' gauge was fascinating, but to be involved in full-size trackwork, even in a junior capacity, at 17 years of age onwards was a totally unexpected aspect of being 'amongst the trams'. An opportunity to carry out a track survey in Leeds now, about fifty years later would be a fine thing! By all the signs it might even come to pass.

Chapter Ten

WIDER HORIZONS

As I have said before I saw very little during the working day of what went on, on the system, during my time of working in the Drawing Office unless we were taken on a job to assist and learn. I realised however that I worked at the hub of the system and that we did get to know about some developments and happenings, though not from an observer's point of view, more from an originator's point of view, thus I took new developments or happenings almost as a matter of course. Old and new secrets were not secrets any more.

For instance, if a Middleton car was seen on any other route than Hunslet or Middleton I knew eventually how, but not why, that had been scheduled and by whom. The fact that a Middleton car was seen on, say, Lawnswood still was a tramway event, but not now quite such an important event as it was in June 1942 when one Middleton car went to Roundhay and Harehills and back each morning. (See Plate 80) Nevertheless in the history of Leeds trams such an occurrence was an event and still is, during reminiscing discussions between people who can say 'I was there!' Nothing, either then or now, detracts from the cars or the Leeds system up to 1945. I got to know the system from the inside as well as the outside. This inside knowledge about 'my' cars and their system that I became privy to always made me feel a privileged person and was what I had been trying for, ever since seeing tramcar 339 in Duncan Street in early 1942.

However, I did get round all the depots and even to Donisthorpe Street Bus Works, though this was mainly on building and civil work. The depot visits answered a lot of seven year-old questions as to where they were and what was in them. There was no thought in those days of a young employee on the staff of Leeds City Transport being given an opportunity, at age 21, to learn to drive a tram or a bus.

Swinegate Depot, now in reverse to Jim Wade's reference to Head Office, was just 'across the road' and, of course, it became very well-known. Chapeltown Depot (and Oliver Anderson) was discovered properly, with its outside siding, on my cycling trips round the City, along with Headingley Depot, adjacent to St. Chad's Road, the location of an awkward siding later on. Bramley and Hunslet Depots along with Stanley Road, though closed now, Torre Road, that treasure-house of historical Leeds cars, the large doorway at the bottom of Sheepshanks Yard, off the top of Vicar Lane (noted particularly during our track survey at North Street/Vicar Lane/New Briggate Junction, Chapter 9), the old depot at Silver Cross Works, Guiseley were part of the 'old world of Leeds trams', although I found no further secrets in any of these places.

Returning to 1944 we learnt fast, both outside on the system and inside about Drawing Office Practice. We learnt to draw properly, print by hand properly, measure up buildings properly and how to conduct ourselves on Tramway Public Duties, i.e. lectures by Tramway Senior Officers and visits to other Departments of the Corporation. These were aspects of City administrative life that were previously completely unknown to me.

Aspects of our own Department in 1944 were that, especially after 6 June, the necessity to be prepared for air raids and their subsequent damage eased considerably. One obvious result to the trams was that the anti-blast netting was gradually removed from the car windows. Post-war thoughts by the Transport Department and Leeds City Council caused Ronnie and I and, indeed, many of the Drawing Office Staff to be part of the production team who prepared drawings for the proposed tramway subways in the centre of Leeds. If these drawings are still in the City Vaults, they will tell the story far better than I can remember what we produced.

One tramcar result of these proposals was that a single-deck bogie car had arrived in Leeds from Sunderland. It was always known as the 'Sunderland Car', never by any of its three numbers, 85, 288 or 600 (Plate 106). None of those numbers fitted with Leeds, at least not in my Leeds-biased mind! We already had an 85, a Piv! 288 was still a balcony car whose number began with a 'magic two' and 600, well, that was past my time, i.e. 1953. The car was given 288 in 1946.

A major event to happen to two Pivotal Cars was that they ceased to be 'Pivotals'. Cars 91 and 147 had their pivotal trucks removed from under their long suffering bodies at Kirkstall Works, and had P.35 trucks fitted. Fancy a Piv., suddenly, after seventeen years, becoming a P.35! P.35s were Horsfields, weren't they? Eventually a considerable number of these truck conversions were effected. First we had 275, 276, and 321 imitating Horsfields by having straight body-sides and, in 276's case, BTH controllers; now we had two Pivs. trying to be Horsfields. But there was no doubt these new trucks improved the Pivs' ride no end. The Horsfields were very, very

Plate 105: Car 600 or the Sunderland car seen (right) at the National Tramway Museum, Crich, Derbyshire on 12 October 1992. Author/National Tramway Museum.

good cars and certainly were worth imitating.

Apart from the cars, sometime in 1944, Stuart Pickford and I volunteered as Auxiliary Conductors. This time the work was not for the trams but for the crews! The routes we volunteered for were the No 3 or 3 Circular to Harehills and Roundhay. We were issued with blue armbands that stated in gold letters; 'L.C.T. Auxiliary Conductor.' We were very proud of our duties which were to assist the regular conductors or conductresses in rush hours, one auxiliary conductor per car. When we boarded the cars, say, at Briggate Barriers our first duty was to ask the regular conductor if we may assist him/her. Usually the answer was 'Yes' especially if we knew the conductor, because we could be of real help on a full car. When the conductor was inside collecting fares or doing likewise upstairs, he/she could not always get back past everybody to the rear platform quick enough to supervise loading or unloading of passengers. A competent auxiliary conductor could stop the dashing about of the conductor who could collect fares and rake the money in for L.C.T. without hassle.

Sometimes, however, a regular conductor did not want any assistance when we asked - for whatever reason (!!) so we either travelled on that car as an ordinary fare-paying passenger or waited for a car whose conductor would like assistance. Fares were not taken by auxiliary conductors and we did not handle money at all. We supervised passengers boarding or alighting from the car, we gave the driver the start or the stop signals plus the 'full-up' and 'emergency stop' signals as required, on the bell-push or the bell-cord. We also had to shout out the name of all the tram-stops, i.e. Shepherd's Lane, Harehills School. Of course, we had to be polite (nearly always) to the passengers as we were representing Leeds City Transport Department and the passengers were paying fares.

An auxiliary conductor's position on the rear platform was under the stairs next to the resistance on some cars with immediate access to the bell-push or cord, but still be accessible near the platform steps to show concern for the passengers. If the regular conductor came back to this position then I would squeeze myself between the controller and the hand-brake pillar and handle (this was usually chained to the window frame out of the way) on a Piv., though still handy for passenger supervision. Sometimes an Inspector got on and then there was congestion on the platform.

Stuart and I flattered ourselves that we knew the No 3 route very well, both into and out of Town, but when one had to deal with the public, in the blackout and under wartime conditions, we found that we had much to learn about individual tramcar operation and, indeed, about public relations. Nevertheless we both enjoyed this bit of official helping-out and we did travel free when doing this duty!

Plate 106: Brian Render wearing an auxiliary Conductor's Armband.
Mrs Annie Render.

However on 2 September, 1944 along with hundreds of other lads, I was required to Register at the Labour Exchange for service in the Forces after our eighteenth birthday. Once this was done and I had admitted my existence to the authorities I knew that it would not be long before I received my Calling-up papers. Sure enough in December the O.H.M.S. envelope came through the letter-box. This instruction insisted that I must report to Caterham Barracks in Surrey by 1600 hours on 11 January, 1945 or else I would be A.W.O.L. from my Regiment-to-be, the Coldstream Guards, having requested to join the Royal Electrical and Mechanical Engineers!

Plate 107: A very sad sight, repeated often in 1945. The old cars that I discovered at Torre Road Top Shed in 1942 along with other balcony cars subsequently taken out of service were taken to Low Fields Road and burned. Car 329 is awaiting its fate in October 1945.
Yorkshire Post.

So came to an end, temporarily I hoped, sixteen months of exciting work at Leeds Tramways and all the years prior to this getting to know the trams and the system. It would all have to stop for, as the Army Pay-book said: 'For the duration of the Emergency' What a sentence! What a Regiment!

For a while, then, goodbye Leeds and 255, 400, 297 and the rest for an unknown length of service well outside my world of Tramways. Hardly had I turned my reluctant back on Leeds to start this new, enforced life in a Regiment which, it was shouted at us, was 'Second to None' (there was no doubt about that!) than I heard that the 'old cars' that were retired to Torre Road Top Shed had been taken to the Mauthausen of tramcars at Low Fields Road and liquidated! After all the romanticising, wondering, imagining, deducing and finally discovering, in 1942, the remaining 'A-cars', the cars whose numbers began with the 'magic two' and most of the balcony cars in the 300's, they had all gone - forever!

I was miles away, confined to training barracks. P.T. every morning and Drill Parades twice a day, running up and down hills, through unimaginable obstacles in order to make us fit - more likely fit-to-drop! What possible chances did I have to save even a number-panel from inside any of the cars? None at all! Could I have saved anything from those cars even if I had still been in Leeds? So frustrating, but I shall never know.

Later in 1945 whilst still under military training, I learnt that there had been a strike of Tramways platform staff and that members of the public had been allowed, or taught, how to drive the trams. By the time I heard about this the strike was over, but in spite of driving the cars in 1942 would I, or any other member of the staff in Head Office, have been allowed to drive the cars? I think not! A member of the staff anywhere near the controls of a tramcar would really have put the cat among the pigeons. What an opportunity disallowed! In 1945 the only tracks I was allowed to drive on were those round the wheels of a Bren-gun carrier!

In 1946 another foreign car arrived in Leeds, this time from Manchester, which added to the anguish caused by the destruction of the balcony cars. This car's number in Manchester was 287 and for a time in Leeds it ran with this Manchester-type number still on its dash. Our 287 was one of the revered balcony cars whose number began with the 'magic two' and was one of those just destroyed.

This foreign 287 wasn't 'magic' at all!

The car's arrival was nothing in comparison to the events of 24 August. On that date my school tram route from Harehills Road via Beckett Street to Town was CLOSED! With it went Stanley Road (the depot had been closed to trams for some time). Buses ran on Harehills Road now!

Such infamy, such sacrilege!! Never again would I hear the points CHLONK-CHLONK at the Sorting Office crossover at Harehills Road. Of course, there were justifiable reasons for the closure of tram routes that were single track and loop lines, but it hurt just the same when I came home on leave and found out about the closures. Another part of the old world of Leeds trams had vanished and to compound the anguish, it had gone within days of another foreign car arriving in the City. We had now tramcar cast-offs from three other systems, London, Hull and Manchester! Where next?

My continuing compulsory world, which lasted just over three years until well after the duration of the emergency, revolved round the Regiment, the training and duty in some well-known locations. Instead of home names like Harehills, Roundhay or Lawnswood it was with great interest, discipline and pride that duties had centred on the various training barracks, then Windsor, The Tower of London, Wellington Barracks, Buckingham Palace and St. James's Palace. A long, long way from Wellington Street and St. James's Hospital!

My only tramway adventure in London was in 1945 when I made the 10 mile journey from Purley to the Embankment and return by Feltham car. We were forbidden to travel to London from Caterham at that time but the Military Police never thought to check the trams! I have only an outline memory of this trip, the trams in London would always be there, wouldn't they, so they could be enjoyed in later years. No one ever supposed that the Felthams would cease to run in London and not for one minute did anyone ever think of Felthams running in LEEDS!

February, 1948 saw my return to the Drawing Office of Leeds City Transport. I considered myself very fortunate to have a job to return to after such an indeterminate period of time away. Nevertheless that return did take some adjustment. I had left the Drawing Office as a junior in 1945 and came back three years older, still as a junior, even though the duties I had been called upon to do in the latter part of those three years had responsibilities far in excess of 'junior' positions.

The old order had changed on the streets. I had changed as well, of course. My horizons were still in London or Windsor or on long marches on the hills. Those horizons were definitely not fetching and carrying tea for people who should have been, but were not, called up.

However, my job was here, still 'amongst the trams' and so I had to discipline myself to accept the return to Drawing Office routine. The trams were just the same, or so I thought, but my home had changed from Harehills to Adel and now my tram route was 1-Lawnswood or West Yorkshire, or Sammy Ledgard's buses. I learnt fairly quickly that, during the time I had been away, other equally interested young people had succumbed to the fascination of Leeds trams and fortunately they had carefully studied and monitored the tramway developments of 1945 to 1948 and which, in later years, they continued to do, very thoroughly. It was very obvious that I would have to do a lot of catching up on Leeds tramcar happenings (as seen from outside the Department) during this period, if I ever could!

Also very obvious to me was the knowledge that no matter how, or if, I caught up, the old world of Leeds trams and with it, my old world, my romantic old world of the cars had, despairingly, gone for ever. 1948 was a year of change for the tramway activities in Leeds. Progression is hardly the correct word, but cost-cutting under the name of improvements made its presence felt in the appearance of the tramcars. This was the time that the trams began to be 'messed-about-with!' The traditional old, characterful look of Leeds Tramways - in my eyes - was gradually changing, not necessarily for the better. The ordinary person had no idea what was proposed or happening behind the scenes of tramway operation. One could only observe the results of the happenings, even though, in my case, I was an employee of the Department.

Cars were coming out of the Paint Shop at K.D. looking entirely different to the old standard Leeds style. Cars that had been on certain routes all their lives were discovered - with some surprise and sometimes with horror - elsewhere on the system. More and more buses, built by the local firm of Charles H Roe at Cross Gates, were coming into service. They were very smooth and smart buses and began to show up 'my' trams as fairly aged, except for the Middleton cars and 272, 273 and 274, of course.

The foreign cars on the system were accepted, after a fashion, in Leeds. The London HR2's, 277, 278 and

Plate 108: A very smooth and smart Leeds bus is illustrated in this advertisement for Charles H. Roe, which appeared in the 1947/1948 Guide to the City of Leeds. Yorkshire Post.

279 were quite good cars really, but the cars from Hull were not worthy, overall, of being called Leeds cars, neither were the hard cases from Manchester. A year later, the rubbish cars that arrived from Southampton were quite out of place no matter how hard the Paint Shop at K.D. tried to make them look like respectable Leeds cars.

The cars from Manchester and Southampton were given numbers between 280 and 300, made vacant by the scrapping of the 'old cars' from the Torre Road Top Shed. This did not endear those foreign cars to me at all. Cars 280 to 300 would always be the 'magic two's to me. Not foreigners!! Even fifty or so years later on 287 is a balcony car, there is no thought of the number being on a foreign car. The shape of Dr Who's Daleks reminded me of the head-on view of those Southampton cars!

Whilst talking about other towns' cars, I am reminded of a present-day error which seems to emanate from heritage-type printers. The proper name for Leeds Tramways was Leeds City Transport Department throughout the time I worked there and right up to its absorption into the Leeds section within the Metropolitan name. There have been various prints, etc., produced in recent years of Horsfield Car 180 as it is at Crich, by certain firms and other descriptions of Leeds cars that have been given the heading of 'Leeds Corporation Tramways - 180', or a similar description of 399 or even 345.

This name of the transport body in Leeds is WRONG!

The Transport Department of Leeds was NEVER known as 'Corporation Transport.' It was always known as Leeds City Transport! The slogan after the war was 'LEEDS LEADS' and we did not follow any other undertakings who used the word 'Corporation' in the title of the Transport Department.

At the same time as things were changing on the tracks in 1948, my Drawing Office training resumed from the break-off point in January, 1945. Ronnie Griffiths and myself ultimately became able to produce drawings that were considered to be of a standard suitable to have come from Leeds City Transport. The standards in the Drawing Office were still of the 'old school', irrespective of the politics of Leeds City Council in relation to the trams, but the Drawing Office Staff were without the guiding hand of Mr Bedell, the Chief Draughtsman who had left Leeds in 1946 to take up another post in Huddersfield. His leaving created a vacancy that was never filled.

However, all the Staff found themselves working flat-out on many different subjects. Sovereign Street Blister Hangar Bus Garage, Bramley Depot conversion to a bus garage, Donisthorpe Street Bus Garage, Stainbeck Lane Siding, St Chad's Siding, an exhibition at Lewis's, and track and site surveys all over the system were just some of the schemes in progress. The Belle Isle-Middleton extension was being built too.

A new tramcar was designed in the Drawing Office and was being built at K.D. in the style of 272, 273 or 274. This was a smoother version of the Austerity car 104 and caused 276, one of the family of special Converts (Chapter 7) to have its number changed from 276 to 342. As a one-off at that time the Leeds City Transport name on both sides of the new 276 was applied in the style of the 1942 letterheads in use in the Department. Not as dignified as the standard white wings and Coat of Arms. The Coat of Arms on 276 was placed on the dash at each end of the car between the headlights.

Plate 109: The LCT logo on their letterhead.
Author

Plate 110: Leeds Coat of Arms by permission of Leeds City Council, Strategic Policy Committee per Ian Walton.

The Sunderland car, now numbered 288, was being prepared for clearance-testing and in my case, night school was resumed at the same time as I started work again in the Drawing Office.

In late June, 1948, I had to be taken to hospital with appendicitis and was eventually transferred to St James's Hospital where, on July 4th, I was very surprised to see Alderman Rafferty, the Chairman of the Transport Committee on Leeds City Council, no less, come into my ward, and in his purposeful way, come to talk to me and ask how I was.

Not content with that visit, two days later he came in again and brought with him Mr W. Vane Morland! I just couldn't believe my eyes! In the 1930s I had seen that name on all the cars and now, 15 years or so later, here was the owner of that name, the person who I thought to be lucky to have his name on all the cars, actually visiting me in hospital. I had never seen Mr W. Vane Morland during my time in the Drawing Office either before or after my army service. It was impossible for me to stand at all, much less to attention, but I was very pleased that the G.M.(he of the little white bulb on the Dictograph) had taken the time to visit one of his junior staff in hospital. I have often wondered since how those two gentlemen knew that one of their junior staff was in St James's. Perhaps that excitement made my stitches become a zip-fastener and made me get better that much quicker? My diary records that three days later the G.M.'s chauffeur brought me a book from the G.M. The book had to be returned, unfortunately.

Further exciting activities later in 1948 were on October 12th, according to my diary. All-night testing of the Sunderland car with Middleton car 265 took place all round the System to check for overhang on tight curves and we took the Sunderland car out again on 28 October at 11.00pm from Swinegate Depot with an accompanying Middleton car on Middleton and also up Belle Isle Road as far as possible. This was the only time, to my knowledge, that two tramcars travelled side by side in the same direction as we returned from the then Belle Isle Road terminus down towards the Balm Road Crossover. The bow collector had to be watched, of course.

We were standing at the front end of the Sunderland car during this unusual experience and it was very obvious that the few motorists and pedestrians coming up Belle Isle Road could not believe their eyes. 'No tramcar comes at me on my side of the road and this is a single-decker! Must have been potent beer in the pub tonight and it's only Thursday night too!'

In August 1949, Mr W. Vane Morland retired as General Manager and Engineer, the new General Manager, a Mr A.B. Findlay, only being appointed in December of that year. We never got to know the new manager and I have no memory of speaking to him. The retirement of Mr Vane Morland seemed to me to coincide with the absolute end of my 'old world' of Leeds trams. The revered 'old cars' had gone and some of the not-so-old cars were being withdrawn, though not necessarily scrapped at once. I questioned our immediate senior officers about this and was told: 'It is none of your business. It is Transport policy.' The 'BLOCK' again! I thought that it was a relief to know that other people, not on the Department, were monitoring current tramcar movements and withdrawals. It was my business!!

In his book 'Leeds Trams 1932 to 1959' Andrew D. Young states that in late 1949, Mr V.J. Matterface, the new Rolling Stock Engineer, Trams, went to London to bring back a London Feltham car, 2099. Now, in spite of working in the Department, I have no memory of even being told about what could have been a most exciting exercise, if we had been asked to assist in some way. Another example of the 'BLOCK' by the establishment??

However, we did assist later when we took 2099 (later 501) 'round the system' at night after the service cars had stopped, along with a Middleton car for clearance tests on tight curves like Moortown Corner. At this particular location I well remember the difficulty of recording the position, on the

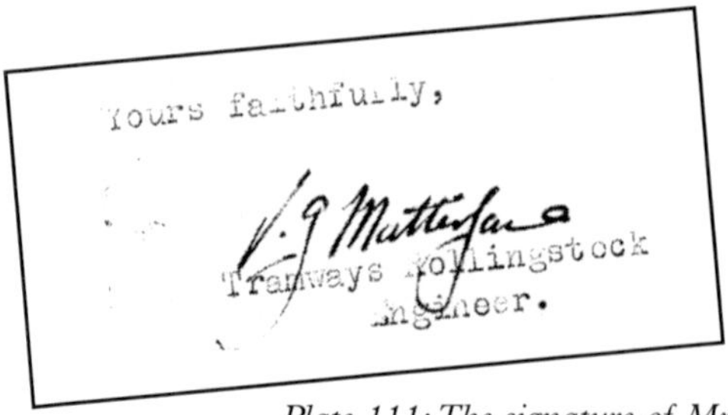

Plate 111: The signature of Mr V.J. Matterface, Rolling Stock Engineer, Trams from a letter to me of 23 November 1951. Author

road surface, of the maximum overhang. i.e the fender. I squashed myself on the bottom doorstep between the centre handrail pillar and the body frame facing into the car, at the 'City End' of the car and with Ronnie Griffiths holding on to me. In this precarious position I reached out holding a piece of hard chalk vertically and put my hand underneath the fender, in vertical line with the maximum swing position of the fender on the road surface (about in line with the bow-rope hanging position).

2099 was driven, slowly of course, from Street Lane round into Harrogate Road, stopped and reversed into Street Lane again with the chalk in my hand under the fender making a line on the road surface as the car went round the curve. The car was then reversed over the crossover in Street Lane adjacent to the Corner (without me!) and brought back, wrong track and watching the bow, into Harrogate Road again.

Someone else then 'walked the car' towards Street Lane with their hand and chalk held on the side of the car on the 'inside' of the outgoing track, vertically in line with the measured centre-line of 2099, round the curve into Street Lane, to face Roundhay. As I remember, these two chalk lines on the road surface were very close and this probably precluded the use of future Feltham cars on the Moortown-Roundhay Circular routes. I always enjoyed unorthodox, though official, activity such as these nocturnal duties, and other adventures organised by or through the Drawing Office.

From mid-1948 in Kirkstall Works the painting experiments that were being made on the trams were supervised by Mr Matterface. These so-called cost-saving experiments with the old blue colours were brought to a head in mid-1950 with the arrival in Leeds of a batch of Feltham cars similar to 2099 and to those that I had ridden on in London in 1945.

Unbelievable!! London would always have its trams, wouldn't it? Yet here they were in Leeds - and still in London Transport red!

The result of these colour experiments in K.D. and the arrival of the red London cars was that 'my' Leeds tramcars were painted red!! The buses were painted green! Red and green were cheaper than blue and would withstand wear and tear better, so we were told. Strangely enough the green suited the buses quite well, but Leeds trams in red - ugh!

The 'Red Period of Deterioration' had started! It would finish only when all the trams had gone from the streets of Leeds in 1959.

Individuality of character and the interest of the cars was lost immediately the red took over. I felt that although I was still living in

Leeds, 'my' trams were now in another town! Whatever must Mr W Vane Morland have thought? Whoever could have imagined a Middleton car with London Transport-style thin numbers, sunken headlights, a miserly destination display and, worst of all, RED paint!!? Never mind the politics or finances, look at the desecration of proper tramcars!

If the colour of Leeds trams and buses had to be changed at all for whatever reason, why couldn't the trams and the buses both have been painted green? Other Corporation-owned vehicles were painted green as a standard colour and once in green the buses always looked smart. The modern buses still do, forty or so years on!

As I have said, my 'old world' of Leeds trams had gone forever in 1945 when the 'A -cars' and the 'magic twos' were scrapped. No matter how difficult or how hard I found it was to accept that reality, the signs were becoming more and more apparent to me that working for and amongst the trams in Leeds would not now be a long-term career project. How things had changed in three or four years! In spite of all the time and effort and excitement in getting to know Leeds cars, their routes, their system, searching for historical cars and driving some of them, all between 1935 and 1943 in readiness for the intended achievement to work 'amongst the trams', the signs seemed to tell me that in the not too distant future I could find myself working amongst the buses - and that would never do! So eventually a move was made into the electricity industry which, with its effects, took me away from Leeds for over thirty years. Perhaps it was as well that I left Leeds because when I play and re-play the video by Leeds Transport Historical Society and see the views of Leeds cars - 'my' cars - being destroyed, I find the scenes heartbreaking.

How could 'they' have done such things to 'my' cars?!!

How could I have let them?!

In May, 1995, during a visit to Leeds to research further photographs (if possible) for this story, I walked down to Swinegate Depot from City Square. I was horrified to find that there was no Swinegate Depot!!

The building, along with Sovereign Street Permanent Way Yard, had been flattened and cleared - to make car parks! There appeared to be nothing whatever left to remind me of all the exciting times spent in these premises between 1940 and 1950. Then I saw the wall! Over there by the railway viaduct was the remains of Pitt Row and next to it a short length of wall. Surely this was the back wall of the Depot?

Plate 112: The inside of Torre Road Top Shed on 14 July 1997 showing the tram tracks of 1942 that were still visible there. Compare the track/car diagram in Plate 70. The Shed was in use as an M.O.T.-type test shed for licensed taxis in Leeds. Author.

Closer inspection of the wall and its position relative to Pitt Row and the 'Arches' confirmed my thoughts. On this wall could just be discerned the faint paint remains of the track numbers of Tracks 18, 19, 20, 21, 22 and 23. Track 23 was where the 'secret' track came out of the Depot and led under the 'Arches'. Now the 'Arches' is a car park too!! Dismayed, I turned my back on this 'wailing wall' and went across to Sovereign Street and then along Concordia Street to the steps of Head Office main entrance, a walk I had done many, many times when working in Head Office. The handrails up the steps were still there, but, looking through the windows at the top of the steps, the building was empty and derelict.

Such a hive of activity for so many years, the Head Office of Leeds City Transport was dead!!

An era had gone and I felt utterly disconsolate having realised that the august body of people of which I had been a part and who had formed the Transport Department through the years had all disappeared.

It was such unbelievable finality and totally irredeemable!!

It is often said that one should not return to places known long ago. This visit to remnants of a first-class tramway system was most upsetting - the old order had vanished! I have found only three remaining traces of the trams in Leeds:-

a. The rails can still be seen in Stanley Road Depot.

b. Torre Road Top Shed, until its demolition in 1998.

c. The 'wailing wall' of Swinegate Depot.

There may, of course, be others of which I am not aware.

I am very well aware, however, that there are two double-deck tramcars from Leeds which in 1959, were rescued from their intended last journey to the scrapyard at Low Fields Road. They have been brought back to life to look and operate as though they were new cars. Their location is at the National Tramway Museum at Crich, Derbyshire.

The cars are:-No. 180, a P.35 or Horsfield, built by Brush at Loughborough in 1931. The car is immaculate in the 1950's red and cream and is 67 years old in 1998, and No. 399, a P.22 or Beeston Air-Brake, built by Leeds City Tramways in 1926. This car, too, is immaculate in the primrose, chocolate and white to show the colours

Plate 113: Car 180, a Horsfield or P.35, the only one of its type left, seen at the National Tramway Museum at Crich, Derbyshire in 1988. In 1988 the car had just been overhauled and has returned to service in immaculate condition. Car 180 is now 68 years old. Author.

Plate 114: Car 399, a P.22 or Beeston Air-Brake, also the only one of its type left, also seen in immaculate condition at the National Tramway Museum on 3 November 1991. The car is painted in chocolate, cream and white, the livery in use in Leeds before 1925. Inset shows Car 380 in service in Leeds in 1925. Car 399 is now 74 years old. Michael Seymour.

Plate 115: Car 345, an ex-balcony car converted to this form about 1938. The car was saved from destruction in 1959 and sent to the National Tramway Museum. It has been under wraps ever since and is waiting for sufficient cash to be raised for it to be refurbished to operating standards and to take its place amongst all the other immaculate tramcars at Crich. Keith Terry.

of Leeds cars before 1925 and is 73 years old in 1998. It is always so exciting and such a pleasure to see, hear and ride on these two cars at Crich (and, with permission, to drive them), even though 180 is in the 1950's red.

At the same time as 180 and 399 were rescued, a third Leeds double-deck tramcar was saved from destruction and brought to Crich. This car is No. 345, (Plate 115), a non-Beeston Convert, originally built by Leeds Tramways about 1921 as a Balcony car and converted by Leeds City Transport to a fully enclosed car possibly in 1937. The car, now 78 years old, has been stored in a 'secret' depot, near Crich for some years and I look forward to the day when, funds permitting, 345 will run at Crich, painted in the true Leeds colours

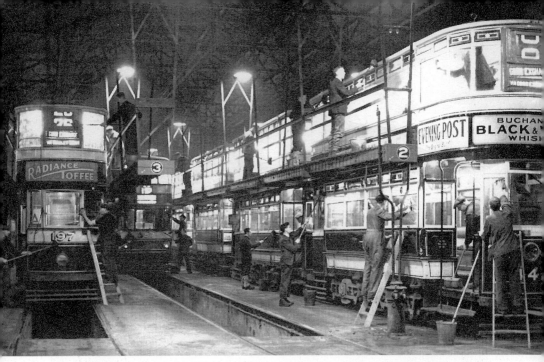

Plate 116: Swinegate Depot about 1938. Another treasure of a photograph, taken possibly at the same time as Plate 41. The cars are on tracks 1, 2 and 3 and the cleaners appear to be the same persons as those in Plate 41. West Yorkshire Archives Service, Wakefield.

of dark blue and cream. (see Chapter 7) An exciting prospect indeed which may bring back other memories of Leeds Tramways' past.

However, my memories of an exciting tramway life cannot be destroyed and so from the mists of my memory between 1926 and 1933 and from unforgettable recollections between 1933 and 1948/1950 here are my lasting impressions of the tramway system Leeds had every reason to be proud of.

With the greatest respect to other tramway systems that I ultimately was able to visit, none had the character of my cars in Leeds and none gave me such perpetual interest and excitement. As long as I live, I shall remember the sound of those crossover points CHLONKING at Harehills Sorting Office and the individual sound of the balcony cars as the driver threw-off for the section-point in Harehills Road near Luxor Avenue and then immediately fed up again, into parallel, to pass the bottom of Milan Road to reach the first stop at Harehills Place.

One other place will always remain prominent in my memory. I felt such tremendous excitement whenever I walked through the main entrance to Swinegate Depot, particularly before 1945, and was able to see the tracks full of cars in 'ranks' of seven or eight, drawn up as on parade, being prepared ready for duty. (Plate 116)